THE DECEPTION OF 666

TERRA KERN

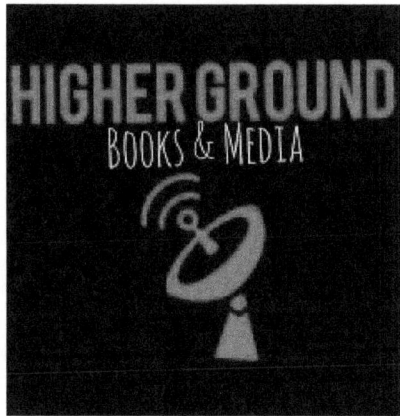

Higher Ground Books & Media
Springfield, Ohio.
http://highergroundbooksandmedia.com

Printed in the United States of America 2022

THE DECEPTION OF 666

TERRA KERN

PREFACE

As I sat down at my computer and pulled out my keyboard with fingers ready to race along the keys to write the fourth book in my The Adventures of Little Jenna Jafferty Series for children, I heard the Spirit speak saying, "Nooo, I want you to write another book for Me." I then asked Him what he wanted me to write about and His answer was 666.

I am not going to lie, I felt completely intimidated as I don't know much about that topic at all. I also know that God indeed knows our hearts and thoughts because without me saying a thing or uttering a word, He told me to just calm down and relax as He wasn't asking me to write about the Book of Revelation, just 666, and to just trust in Him and He would lead me in what He wanted written. He explained that He would give me some Scriptures to study and show me hints all through His Word. That calmed my troubled soul because I was in fact fretting over and thinking He wanted me to write on the whole Book of Revelation.

The above-mentioned incident sent me on my journey of writing this book. Through many days, weeks, and months of prayer and seeking Him, He took me on a journey beginning from before He set and laid out the foundation of the earth, explaining all of this needs to be understood before we can understand the deception of 666. All of what He has revealed to me is within the pages of this book as He has asked of me. I have found all of it to be truly amazing and not at all what my mind was conditioned to believe in times past according to the traditions of men and philosophies and doctrines of demons that have infiltrated the church, as we are indeed in a season where God is shining His light of revelation on the darkness of philosophies, doctrines of demons, and the traditions of men.

The Lord also gave me encouragement and confirmation along the way as I discovered others were receiving the same revelations from God. His Word does say in 2 Corinthians 13:1 that by the mouth of two or three witnesses every word shall be established. And therefore, the Bible interprets itself. Thank you, Father! I find all of this to be truly humbling! God's goodness is beyond measure!

Revelation 13:16-18 – He causes all, both small and great, rich and poor, free and slave, to receive a mark on their right hand or on their foreheads, and that no one may buy or sell except one who has the mark or the name of the beast, or the number of his name. Here is wisdom. Let him who has understanding calculate the number of the beast, for it is the number of a man: His number is 666.

Revelation 7:2-3 – Then I saw another angel ascending from the east having the seal of God. And he cried with a loud voice to the four angels to whom it was granted to harm the earth and the sea, saying, "Do not harm the earth, the sea, or the trees till we have sealed the servants of our God on their foreheads.

Colossians 2:8 – Beware lest anyone cheat you through philosophy and empty deceit, according to the tradition of men, according to the basic principles of the world, and not according to Christ.

1 Timothy 4:1-2 – Now the Spirit expressly says that in the latter times, some will depart from the faith, giving heed to deceiving spirits and doctrines of demons, speaking lies in hypocrisy, having their own conscious seared with a hot iron.

2 Thessalonians 2:3-4 – Let no one deceive you by any means; for that Day will not come unless the falling away comes first, and the man of sin is revealed, the son of perdition, who opposes and exalts himself above all that is called God or that is worshipped, so that he sits as God, in the temple of God, showing himself that he is God.

It is my prayer that as you read the pages of this book, that your heart would be completely open to what the Holy Spirit is revealing and teaching.

CHAPTER ONE

BEFORE THE FOUNDATION OF THE WORLD

Before time as we know it even began, God had a plan for the earth and those who inhabit it. He preordained and predestined the events that would take place on it, the people who would be involved, whether good or evil, and the times in which those events would take place as well which people would be living in those particular times. He waited for certain things to reach a particular point before He moved on the earth with the beginning of the next stage or new season, and then He set it forth in motion. These things the Lord showed me caused my heart to leap for joy and at times, caused tears of gratitude to uncontrollably flow from my eyes, caused my faith to grow even stronger, as well as caused me to become completely awestricken. I am so excited to share these things with you and pray they will have the same impact on you.

Let's take a look at a sampling of Scriptures that show Father God had a plan and purpose for everything before He even laid the foundation of the earth.

Job 38:4 – "Where were you when I laid the foundations of the earth? Tell Me if you have understanding."

Isaiah 44:24-27 - Thus says the Lord, your Redeemer, and He who formed you from the womb: "I, the LORD, who makes all things, Who stretches out the heavens all alone, Who spreads abroad the earth by Myself, Who frustrates the signs of the babblers, And drives diviners mad; Who turns wise men backward, And makes their knowledge foolishness; Who confirms the word of His servant, And performs the counsel of His messengers; Who says to Jerusalem, 'You shall be inhabited," To the cities of Judah, 'You shall be built,' And I will raise up her waste places; Who says to the deep, 'Be dry! And I will dry up your rivers;'"

Isaiah 45:11-13 – Thus says the LORD, The Holy One of Israel, and Maker: "Ask Me of things to come concerning My sons; and concerning the work of My hands, you command Me. I have made the earth, and created man on it. I—My hands—stretched out the heavens, and all their host I have commanded."

Isaiah 46:9-10 – …I am God, and there is no other; I am God and there is none like Me, Declaring the end from the beginning, And from ancient times things that are not yet done, Saying, My counsel shall stand, And I will do all my pleasure,

Matthew 13:35 – that it might be fulfilled which was spoken by the prophet saying: "I will open my mouth in parables; I will utter things kept secret from the foundation of the world."

Matthew 25:34 – "Then the King will say to those on His right hand, 'Come, you blessed of My Father, inherit the kingdom prepared for you from the foundation of the world:'"

John 17:24 – "Father, I desire that they also whom You gave Me may be with Me where I am, that they may behold My glory which You have given Me; For You loved Me before the foundation of the world."

Let me pause here for just a moment. Did you catch that? Just as God gave us Jesus as a gift, God also gave us to Jesus. God gave us to Jesus! Jesus said, "…that they also whom *You gave Me*…" Doesn't that just make your heart soar and overflow? Doesn't it just inspire you to be all that He has called you to be and do everything He has planned for you and your life? I know because He gave me to Jesus, I want to be the best gift that I can be. I recognize that I can only do that by being obedient to the Lord and allowing Him to work in and through me. Hallelujah! Okay, let's continue on.

Acts 15:18 – "Known to God from eternity are all His works."

Ephesians 1:4-5 – just as He chose us in Him before the foundation of the world, that we should be holy and without blame before Him in love, having predestined us to adoption as sons by Jesus Christ to Himself, according to the good pleasure of His will,

Ephesians: 1:10-11 – In Him also we have obtained an inheritance, being predestined according to the counsel of His will, that in the dispensation of the fullness of the times He might gather together in one all things in Christ, both which are in heaven and which are in earth—in Him.

Ephesians 2:10 – For we are His workmanship, created in Christ Jesus for good works, which God prepared beforehand that we should walk in them.

2 Timothy 1:9 – who has saved us and called us with a holy calling, not according to our works, but according to His own purpose and grace which was given to us in Christ Jesus before time began,

Hebrews 1:10-12 – And: "You, LORD, in the beginning laid the foundation of the earth, And the heavens are the work of your hands. They will perish, but You remain; And they will all grow old like a garment; Like a cloak You will fold them up, And they will be changed. But You are the same, And Your years will not fail.

Hebrews 4:3 – …although the works were finished from the foundation of the world.

Hebrews 9:26 – He then would have had to suffer often since the foundation of the world; but now, once at the end of the ages, He has appeared to put away sin by the sacrifice of Himself.

1 Peter 1:2 – elect according to the foreknowledge of God the Father, in sanctification of the Spirit, for obedience and sprinkling of the blood of Christ:

1 Peter 1:20 – He indeed was foreordained before the foundation of the world, but was manifest in these last times for you.

Revelation 13:8 – All who dwell on the earth will worship him, whose names have not been written in the Book of Life of the Lamb slain from the foundation of the world.

So we learn that Father God had an explicit plan and purpose before He even laid out the foundation of the world, before He even created the earth. That plan also included each and every one of us and every person who has lived, as well as every person who is yet to live. Here are some more Scriptures that show us this.

Job 10:11 – Your hands have made me and fashioned me, an intricate unity; …Did You not…Clothe me with skin and flesh and knit me together with bones and sinews?

Psalm 139:13-16 – "For You formed my inward parts; You covered me in my mother's womb. I will praise You, for I am fearfully and wonderfully made; Marvelous are Your works, And that my soul knows very well. My frame was not hidden from You, When I was made in secret, And skillfully wrought in the lowest parts of the earth. Your eyes saw my substance, being yet unformed. And in your book they are all written, The days fashioned for me, When as yet there were none of them.

Jeremiah 1:5 – "Before I formed you in the womb, I knew you; before you were born I sanctified you; I ordained you a prophet to the nations."

Luke 1:15 – For he shall be great in the sight of the Lord…He will also be filled with the Holy Spirit, even from his mother's womb.

Roman's 9:11-12 – (for the children not yet being born, nor having done any good or evil, that the purpose of God according to election might stand, not of works but of Him who calls), it was said to her, "The older shall serve the younger."

Next, He showed me that over and beyond that, He predestined certain things would happen at certain times as His plan and time progressed and unfurled. Let's take a look at some of those Scriptures.

Genesis 15:16 – But in the fourth generation they shall return here, for the iniquity of the Amorites is not yet complete."

2 Chronicles 10:15 – So the king did not listen to the people; for the turn of events was from God, that the LORD might fulfill His Word, which He had spoken by the hand of Ahijah the Shilonite to Jereboam the son of Nebat.

Ecclesiastes 3:1 – To everything there is a season, a time for every purpose under heaven:

Ecclesiastes 3:17 – I said in my heart, "God shall judge the righteous and the wicked, For there is a time there for every purpose and for every work."

Ecclesiastes 8:6 – Because for every matter there is a time and judgment, though the misery of man increases greatly.

Isaiah 14:24 – The LORD of hosts has sworn, saying, "Surely, as I have thought, so it shall come to pass, and as I have purposed, so it shall stand."

Habakkuk 2:3 – For the vision is yet for an appointed time; but at the end it will speak, and it will not lie. Though it tarries, wait for it; because it will surely come, it will not tarry.

Acts 13:48 – Now when the Gentiles heard this, they were glad and glorified the word of the Lord. And as many as had been appointed to eternal life believed.

Acts 17:26-27 – "And He has made from one blood every nation of men to dwell on all the face of the earth, and has determined their preappointed times and the boundaries of their dwellings, so that they should seek the Lord, in the hope that they might grope for Him and find Him, though He is not far from each one of us;"

Galatians 4:4 – But when the fullness of the time had come, God sent forth His Son, born of a woman, born under the law,

Romans 8:29-30 – For whom He foreknew, He also predestined to be conformed to the image of His Son, that He might be the firstborn among many brethren. Moreover, whom He predestined, these He also called; whom He called, these He also justified; and whom He justified, these He also glorified.

Romans 11:2 – God has not cast away His people whom He foreknew…

Romans 11:25 – For I do not desire, brethren, that you should be ignorant of this mystery, lest you should be wise in your own opinion, that blindness in part has happened to Israel until the fullness of the Gentiles has come in.

Ephesians 1:5 – having predestined us to adoption as sons by Jesus Christ to Himself, according to the good pleasure of His will.

Ephesians 1:11 – In Him also we have obtained an inheritance, being predestined according to the purpose of Him who works all things according to the counsel of His will,

Revelation 17:17 – "for God has put it into their hearts to fulfill His purpose, to be of one mind, and to give their kingdom to the beast, until the words of God are fulfilled."

The Lord showed me that it is of utmost importance that we understand that He created all beings and things, everything that exists, both good and evil, for His good purposes, in order for us to understand about 666, the number of man, which we will dig into later on in forthcoming chapters. But for now, let's look at some of the Scriptures that tell us He created every single thing.

Proverbs 16:4 – The Lord has made all for Himself, yes, even the wicked for the day of doom.

Isaiah 45:7 – I form the light and create darkness, I make peace and create calamity; I the LORD do all these things. The KJV says it like this – "I form the light, and create darkness: I make peace, and create evil: I the LORD do all these things."

Isaiah 54:16 – "Behold, I have created the blacksmith who blows the coals in the fire, who brings forth an instrument for his work; and I have created the spoiler to destroy."

Daniel 7:27 – Then the kingdom and dominion, And the greatness of the kingdoms under the whole heaven, Shall be given to the people, the saints of the Most High. His kingdom is an everlasting kingdom, And all dominions shall serve and obey Him.

Amos 3:6 – If a trumpet is blown in a city, will not the people be afraid? If there is calamity in a city, will not the LORD have done it?

Micah 1:12 – For the inhabitant of Maroth pined for good, but disaster came down from the LORD to the gate of Jerusalem.

Micah 2:3 – Therefore thus says the LORD: "Behold, against this family I am devising disaster, from which you cannot remove your necks; nor shall you walk haughtily, for this is an evil time."

Romans 8:38-39 – For I am persuaded that neither death nor life, nor angels nor principalities nor powers, nor things present nor things to come, nor height nor depth, nor any other created thing, shall be able to separate us from the love of God…

Romans 9:22-23 – What if God, wanting to show His wrath and to make His power known, endured with much longsuffering the vessels of wrath prepared for destruction, and that He might make known the riches of His glory on the vessels of mercy, which He had prepared beforehand for glory,

Ephesians 1:10-11 – that in the dispensation of the fullness of the times He might gather together in one all things in Christ, both which are in heaven, and which are on earth—in Him. In Him also we have obtained an inheritance, being predestined according to the purpose of Him who works all things according to the counsel of His will,

1 Colossians 1:16 – For by Him all things were created that are in heaven and that are on earth, visible and invisible, whether thrones or dominions or principalities or powers. All things were created through Him and for Him.

Remember, Ephesians 6:12 says, For we do not wrestle against flesh and blood but against principalities, against powers, against the rulers of the darkness of this age, against spiritual hosts of wickedness in the heavenly places. And Paul teaches in Ephesians 3:9-11 – and to make all see what is the fellowship of the mystery, which from the beginning of the ages has been hidden in God who created all things through Jesus Christ; to the intent that now the manifold wisdom of God might be made known by the church to the principalities and powers in the heavenly places, according to the eternal purpose which He accomplished in Christ Jesus our Lord.

So, wait! What? Am I saying that God created both good and evil? Well, they both fall under "all" things, don't they? The Scriptures teach that the devil is evil, don't they? They say he came to kill, steal and destroy. Those things are evil are they not? Demons and the devil's angels also are evil beings as well and fall under "all" things as do all human beings. In times past and even today, this has been a stumbling block causing the question of how a loving God could create or allow evil. And right here is where we need to stop questioning God. He does indeed address this in His Word.

Romans 9:17-23 reads, For the scripture says to the Pharaoh, "For this very purpose I have raised you up, that I may show My power in you, and that My name may be declared in all the earth." Therefore, He has mercy on whom He wills, and whom He wills He hardens. You will say to me then, "Why does He still find fault? For who has resisted His will?" But indeed, O man, who are you to reply against God? Will the thing formed say to Him who formed it, "Why have you made me like this?" Does not the potter have power over the clay, from the same lump to make one vessel for honor and another for dishonor? What if God, wanting to show His wrath and to make His power known, endured with much longsuffering the vessels of wrath prepared for destruction, and that He might make known the riches of His glory on the vessels of wrath prepared for destruction,

And 2 Timothy 2:20 reads, "But in a great house there are not only vessels of gold and silver, but also of wood and clay, some for honor and some for dishonor." Proverbs 16:4 says, The Lord has made all for Himself, Yes, even the wicked for the day of doom. Isaiah 45:9 says, "Woe to him who strives with his Maker! Let the potsherd strive with the potsherds of the earth! Shall the clay say to him who forms it, 'What are you making?' Or shall your handiwork say, 'He has no hands'?"

As a matter of fact, when Job questioned God, God in turn asked questions of Job in Job chapters 38 through 41. There are way too many to list them all, but here is a sampling of them just so that we may get God's point. "Have you ever in your life commanded the morning,
And caused the dawn to know its place, That it might take hold of the ends of the earth, And the wicked be shaken out of it?" "Have the gates of death been revealed to you, or have you seen the gates of deep darkness?" "Have you entered the storehouses of the snow, or have you seen the storehouses of the hail, which I have reserved for the time of distress, for the day of war and battle?" "Who has put wisdom in the innermost being or given understanding to the mind?" "Who provides food for the raven when its young ones cry to God and wander about for lack of food?" "Will you really annul My judgment? Will you condemn Me that you may be justified?" Did you catch that? God asks, "Will you really annul My judgment? Will you condemn Me that you may be justified?"

I'm quite confident that God has made His point precisely in why we shouldn't question Him as to why He does things the way He does them, because as He says in Isaiah 55:9 – For as the heavens are higher than the earth, So are My ways higher than your ways, And My thoughts than your thoughts.

So, what then? Am I saying that God created some of mankind to burn in hell throughout eternity? Absolutely not! We are all familiar with John 3:16 – For God so loved the world that He gave His only begotten Son, that whoever believes in Him should not perish but have everlasting life. And 2 Peter 3:9 – The Lord is not slack concerning His promise, as some count slackness, but is longsuffering toward us, not willing that any should perish but that all should come to repentance.

Now some may ask well, that's in the New Testament, what about those who lived before then? We can turn to the Old Testament and find the same thing. Isaiah 59:1 says, Behold, the LORD's hand is not shortened, that it cannot save; nor His ear heavy, that it cannot hear. And we find in Ezekiel 18:21-23 that God says, "But if a wicked man turns from all his sins which he has committed, keeps all my statutes, and does what is lawful and right, he shall surely live; he shall not die. None of the transgressions which he has committed shall be remembered against him; because of the righteousness which he has done, he shall live. Do I have any pleasure at all the wicked should die?" says the LORD GOD, "and not that he should turn from his ways and live?" We also have Ezekiel 33:11 – "Say to them: 'As I live,' says the LORD GOD, 'I have no pleasure in the death of the wicked, but that the wicked turn from his way and live. Turn, turn from your evil ways! For why should you die...?'"

We further learn that the lake of fire was never intended for man at all in Matthew 25:41 – "Then He will also say to those on the left hand, 'Depart from Me, you cursed, into everlasting fire prepared for the devil and his angels:'" This reiterates God's desire that no one should die in sin. But because Satan's evil heart doesn't want to be there in the lake of fire for all of eternity with his own angels only, he tries to deceive the whole world in order to take them with him. God has made a way of escape, but unfortunately, many will scoff and reject it and indeed be cast into the lake of fire as is revealed in Revelation 20:15 – And anyone not found written in the Book of Life was cast into the lake of fire. We'll discuss this in more depth in an upcoming chapter, but I just wanted to highlight that God's intentions are that no one should die in sin and He has indeed made a way of escape.

Each and every person God created to show His glory through, throughout the whole Bible, had an opportunity to turn from their wickedness, by faith, after God did show His glory through them, as well as any others who saw it, once God's glory was revealed. In Exodus, Moses said anyone who wanted to come with them had to follow the commands and statutes of God and it says a little later that a mixed multitude left Egypt. Through faith, Rahab, the prostitute saved herself and her family in the Book of Joshua and she is commended for doing so in Hebrews 11:31 – "By faith the harlot Rahab did not perish with those who did not believe, when she had received the spies with peace." And she became part of Jesus' lineage as Matthew 1:5 shows us. "Salmon begot Boaz by Rahab, Boaz begot Obed by Ruth, Obed begot Jesse." And speaking of Ruth, Ruth chose to follow her mother-in-law Naomi's God rather than return to her people and their gods, after Naomi encouraged her to do so. Ruth 1:16-17 reads, But Ruth said, " Entreat me not to leave you, or turn back from following you; For wherever you go, I go; And wherever you lodge, I will lodge; Your people shall be my people, And your God, my God. Where you die, I will die, and there be buried. The LORD do so to me, and more also, If anything but death parts you and me." All of the above-mentioned people had a choice just as we do today.

From a human perspective, yes, things in this world go awry, dreadfully awry. But we need to see through God's perspective.

Things do not "go awry" unless God "determines beforehand" that they go awry or get off kilter. It's merely God's plan from the beginning. See, God created the wicked one, evil Satan, that serpent of old, to be His sub-ordinate, His assistant or the vehicle in which He uses to bring about His good purposes on the earth as things go awry, in order to show the whole earth His glory. God uses evil to bring His purposes to pass, to make a stark contrast between Himself and His ways, and the enemy and his ways, in order for mankind to see and seek and desire and choose Him.

How can we desire and choose light if there is no darkness? How can we desire and choose love without hatred? How can we desire and choose peace without calamity, chaos, and turmoil? How can we desire and choose healing without disease and sickness? How can we desire and choose freedom without bondage? How can we desire and choose blessings without curses? How can we desire and choose wholeness without brokenness? How can we choose and desire God's truth if we don't have the devil's lies? How can we choose anything without choices? We can't. This is why before God even laid the foundation of the earth, He had a plan. Let us praise and thank our Father God for it, in Jesus' name! Amen!

CHAPTER TWO

GOD'S SOVEREIGNTY AND STAYING POWER

As I was praying and seeking the Lord regarding the writing of this book, He kept showing me Scriptures that point to Him being all knowing and His ways beyond our comprehension. I sensed He wanted us to know just as Paul says in 1 Corinthians 13:12 – "For now we see in a mirror, dimly, but then face to face. Now I know in part, but then I shall know just as I also am known.", that there are some things we simply cannot understand in the here and now and He doesn't want those things to be stumbling blocks to us. We must understand these things before we delve into understanding 666.

As we touched on in chapter one, Isaiah 55:9 says – For as the heavens are higher than the earth, So are My ways higher than your ways, And My thoughts than your thoughts". And there are other Scriptures that teach us the same thing. Proverbs 14:12 says, "There is a way that seems right to a man, but its end is the way of death." Also in Proverbs, we find chapter 21, verse 2 that states "Every way of a man is right in his own eyes, but the LORD weighs the hearts." Then in Romans 11:33 we learn "Oh, the depth of the riches both of the wisdom and knowledge of God! How unsearchable are His judgments and His ways past finding out!"

See, we have been given the mind of Christ if we've trusted in Him and we're new creations in Him, as 2 Corinthians 5:17 says, "Therefore, if anyone is in Christ, he is a new creation; old things have passed away; behold, all things have become new." And again in 1 Corinthians 2:16 – For "who has known the mind of the LORD that he may instruct Him?" But we have the mind of Christ. – However, even with the mind of Christ, God's thoughts are far beyond our thoughts. David admits in Psalm 139:6, "Such knowledge is too wonderful for me; it is high, I cannot attain it." We can't understand everything God is doing, as Solomon wrote in

Ecclesiastes 3:11, "He has made everything beautiful in its time. Also, He has put eternity in their hearts, except that no one can find out the work that God does from beginning to end." And in Isaiah 40:28, we find – "Have you not known? Have you not heard? The everlasting God, the LORD, the creator of the ends of the earth, neither faints nor is weary. His understanding is unsearchable."

God our Father is letting us know that there are some mysteries that we just don't get to know because His ways are past finding out, however, He does give us understanding in part and in season. I hear the Spirit saying that He wants us to understand that He has complete sovereignty over all things, including evil, disaster, and calamity, and has from the very beginning. God the Father, God the Son, and God the Holy Spirit was in the beginning and has been to the end and back.

God wants us to know there is a creature that exists whose name means accuser, a devil which means slanderer, a deceiver of the whole world. He tells us this in Revelation 12:7-9 – And war broke out in heaven: Michael and his angels fought with the dragon; and the dragon and his angels fought, but they did not prevail, nor was a place found for them in heaven any longer. So the great dragon was cast out, that serpent of old, called the devil and Satan, who deceives the whole world; he was cast to the earth, and his angels with him. And Jesus told seventy of His disciples that He witnessed the fall in Luke 10:18 – And He said to them, "I saw Satan fall like lightening from heaven." And notice what He says next in verse 19 – "Behold, I give you the authority to trample on serpents and scorpions, and over all the power of the enemy, and nothing shall by any means hurt you." Hallelujah! Thank you, Jesus!

God wants us to know there is a ruler of this world as it says in John 12:31 – "Now is the judgment of this world; now the ruler of this world will be cast out." And in John 14:30 – "I will no longer talk much with you, for the ruler of this world is coming, and he has nothing on Me." as well as in John 16:11 – "of judgment, because the ruler of this world is judged." God also wants us to understand that there is a god of this age as it states in 2 Corinthians 4:4 – "whose minds the god of this age has blinded, who do not believe, lest the light of the gospel of the glory of Christ, who is the image of God, should shine on them." He wants us to know there is a prince of the power of the air as is taught in Ephesians 2:2 – "in which you once walked according to the course of this world according to the prince of the power of the air, the spirit who now works in the sons of disobedience," God wants us to realize that there is a Beelzebub, the ruler of demons as we learn about in Matthew 12:24 – Now when the Pharisees heard it they said, "This fellow does not cast out demons except by Beelzebub, the ruler of the demons."

God wants us to know all of this, but He also wants us to know that He is sovereign over this being and his hordes of demons and they are only allowed to do what He allows them to do. Period! And He only allows them to work evil so that God can then turn it around for our own good and His good purposes as we are trained and taught by His Holy Spirit, to bring us to perfection, as well as to bring about what He has predestined for us, making His glory known through us.

He shows us His sovereignty over Satan many times throughout His Word. He wants us to know that although the devil is the ruler of this world, it says in Daniel 4:17 – "…The Most High rules in the kingdom of men…" He wants us to see that although unclean spirits are everywhere doing dastardly and deceptive things, that our Jesus has all authority over them as Mark 1:27 says, "For with authority He commands even the unclean spirits, and they obey Him." God wants us to understand that although the devil walks about as a roaring lion seeking someone to devour from 1 Peter 5:8, that in 1 Peter 5:9, Peter says that the sharp teeth of this lion are, in actuality, the sufferings of persecution: "Resist him steadfast in the faith, knowing that the same sufferings are experienced by your brotherhood in the world." And that Peter already stated in 1 Peter 3:17 that this suffering doesn't happen outside of God's sovereign will. "For it is better to suffer for doing good than for doing evil if it happens to be the will of God.

God wants us to recognize that as in 2 Corinthians 4:4, Satan has blinded the eyes of unbelievers, but that a couple of verses later, it is He who eliminates that blindness. 2 Corinthians 4:6 – "For it is the God who commanded light to shine out of darkness, who has shone in our hearts to give the light of the knowledge of the glory of God in the face of Jesus Christ." Our Father in heaven also wants us to realize that when Satan desired to destroy Job, to reveal that God was not the greatest treasure of Job's heart, he had to ask permission to attack him and God allowed him to but set boundaries in what he could do. God said Satan could not touch Job's body and Satan destroyed everything around him. Then again God set the parameters of what Satan could do. He commanded that he could afflict Job's body but could not take his life in Job 1:2 and Job 2:6. Satan could only do what God allowed him to do and in the end as Job proved that God was indeed the utmost treasure of Job's heart, God blessed him with a double portion of all he had lost. Satan was just a vehicle to bring Job to that place of understanding God even more and the double portion blessing that followed.

We need to understand that Satan wants us to sin. He is the great tempter. Luke 22:31 says, – and the Lord said, "Simon, Simon! Indeed Satan has asked for you, that he may sift you as wheat." Notice Satan had to ask permission to tempt Peter into failure, to shake him as in a sieve like it says in Amos 9:9 – "For surely I will command, and will sift the house of Israel among all nations, as grain is sifted in a sieve..." But also note that Jesus has sovereignty over the devil and the outcome of the tempting. He says in verse 32 – "But I have prayed for you, that your faith should not fail; and when you have returned, strengthen your brethren." Did you catch that? Jesus said "when" you return, not "if" you return. See, Jesus rules over all of Satan's designs and tempting. Satan wanted Peter to be shaken up and fail, but Jesus sets out to have Peter become forged into a powerful mature leader.

In John 8:44 Jesus states that the devil was a murderer from the beginning. But God has final authority over who lives or doesn't as found in James 4:15 – "...If the Lord wills, we shall live and do this or that." This is another example of God having sovereignty and ruling over Satan and his minions. And again, Daniel 7:27 says …And all dominions shall serve and obey Him.

Now that we have shown that God is sovereign over the enemy and evil spirits, let's look at some examples of Him ruling evil spirits in the Scriptures. Judges 8:33 says – So it was, as soon as Gideon was dead, that the children of Israel again played the harlot with the Baals, and made Baal-Berith their god. Judges 9:1-4 reads – Then Abimelech the son of Jerubbaal went to Shechem, to his mother's brothers, and spoke with them and with all the family of the house of his mother's father, saying, "Please speak in the hearing of all the men of Shechem: 'Which is better for you, that all seventy of the sons of Jerubbaal reign over you, or that one reign over you?' Remember that I am your own flesh and bone." And his mother's brothers spoke all these words concerning him in the hearing of all the men of Shechem; and their heart was inclined to follow Abimelech, for they said, "He is our brother."

See, after Gideon died, Abimelech desired power and as a result, enticed the citizens of Shechem to accept his rule over them by implying that he cared for them since they were his relatives. Then in the rest of chapter 9, we find that after he was made their king, he hired "worthless and reckless men" and proceeded to murder some of the members of his own family. Then after three years of Abimelech's evil reign, God decided to eradicate him and sent an evil spirit to create conflict between him and the citizens and He used that evil spirit to accomplish His will. Judges 9:23 says – God sent a spirit of ill will between Abimelech and the men of Shechem; and the men of Shechem dealt treacherously with Abimelech.

Later in the Scriptures, we read that God also sent a distressing spirit to terrorize King Saul in 1 Samuel 16:14-16 – But the Spirit of the LORD departed from Saul, and a distressing spirit from the LORD troubled him. And Saul's servants said to him, "Surely a distressing spirit from God is troubling you. Let our master now command your servants, who are before you, to seek out a man who is a skillful player on the harp. And it will be that he shall play it with his hand when the distressing spirit from God is upon you, and you shall be well." This occurred because King Saul had disobeyed and sinned before God in 1 Samuel 15 and his throne was going to be removed from him.

And again, we find God sending the distressing spirit in 1 Samuel 18:10 – And it happened on the next day that the distressing spirit from God came upon Saul, and he prophesied inside the house. So David played music with his hand, as at other times; but there was a spear in Saul's hand. And in 1 Samuel 19:9 – Now the distressing spirit from the LORD came upon Saul as he sat in his house with his spear in his hand. And David was playing music with his hand. So, once more we see that evil angels were used by God to accomplish His will. On this occasion they were used to discipline Saul for being disobedient to the LORD's command.

Next, we'll take a look at 1 Kings, chapter 22 where we find another occasion when God used a lying spirit to discipline someone for his sin. And that is the wicked King Ahab. King Ahab, the king of Israel, had just asked the king of Judea, Jehoshaphat, if he would partner with him and go to war against the nation of Aram. The prophets of the land had been brought before the kings and every one of them declared that God would grant them victory. King Ahab was desperate for the truth though, so he finally asked for the prophet Micaiah. Micaiah was a true prophet of God, not like the others. In 1 Kings 22:13-14 the messenger that was sent to Micaiah encouraged him to prophesy favorably, like all the other prophets. But Micaiah prophesied as God had instructed him.

So, Micaiah warned the king in 1 Kings 22:19-23 – Then Micaiah said, "Therefore hear the word of the LORD: I saw the LORD sitting on His throne, and all the host of heaven standing by, on His right hand and on His left. And the LORD said, 'Who will persuade Ahab to go up, that he may fall at Ramoth Gilead?' So one spoke in this manner, and another spoke in that manner. Then a spirit came forward and stood before the LORD and said, 'I will persuade him.' The LORD said to him, 'In what way?' So, he said, 'I will go out and be a lying spirit in the mouth of all his prophets.' And the LORD said, 'You shall persuade him, and also prevail. Go out and do so.' Therefore look! The LORD has put a lying spirit in the mouth of all these prophets of yours, and the LORD has declared disaster against you." And just as God had proclaimed through His true prophet, Ahab was defeated in battle in 1 Kings 22:29-40.

God also desires for us to realize that He indeed has staying power over us, His children. He wants us to understand that He most certainly wields His influence with us, to keep us safe while serving, worshipping and praising Him forever and ever. Let's take a look at some Scriptures that teach us just that.

Jeremiah 32:40 – And I will make an everlasting covenant with them, that I will not turn away from doing them good; but I will put My fear in their hearts so that they will not depart from Me.

Ezekiel 36:27 – "I will put My spirit within you; and cause you to walk in My statutes, and you will keep My judgments and do them."

1 Corinthians 1:8-9 – Who will also confirm you to the end, that you may be blameless in the day of our Lord Jesus Christ. God is faithful, by whom you were called into the fellowship of His Son, Jesus Christ our Lord.

Philippians 1:6 – Being confident of this very thing, that He who has begun a good work in you will complete it until the day of Jesus Christ;

Philippians 2:13,15 – for it is God who works in you both to will and to do for His good pleasure…that you may become blameless and harmless, children of God without fault in the midst of a crooked and perverse generation, among whom you shine as lights in the world.

Hebrews 13:20-21 – Now may the God of peace who brought up our Lord Jesus from the dead, that great Shepherd of the sheep, through the blood of the everlasting covenant, make you complete in every good work to do His will, working in you what is well pleasing in His sight, through Jesus Christ, to whom be glory forever and ever. Amen.

Now that we've learned of God's sovereignty over the devil and his evil hordes as well as His staying power to keep us in Him, we now need to see His sovereignty over every single thing on earth and in the entire universe. God's sovereignty, His supremacy over the entire works of His hands is dramatically depicted in the Scriptures. It doesn't matter whether it's members of mankind, inanimate objects, or creatures wild and free. They all do God's will at His command.

In Exodus chapter 14, we find the Red Sea split in half and become tall water walls allowing His people to pass through upon His bidding. Then there's Numbers chapter 14 where we find the earth opening her mouth to swallow up the all the rebels, causing them all to tumble into the pit at God's order. Then, when commanded, the sun stood still in its place in Joshua 10. Another example of God's sovereignty over the sun is found in Isaiah 38:8 when it went backward ten degrees on Ahaz's dial. Or how about when God exercised His supreme sovereignty over ravens, willing them to feed his prophet Elijah in 1 Kings 17, and then again in 2 Kings 6:5-6 where He causes an iron ax head to float on top of the water.

Although God's sovereignty is revealed from cover to cover throughout the whole Bible, we will mostly focus on the Psalms and the book of Daniel as they show it in abundance. But before we do that, let's first look at 1 Chronicles 29:11-12 – Yours, O LORD, is the greatness, the power and the glory, the victory and the majesty; for all that is in earth is Yours; Yours is the kingdom, O LORD, and You are exalted as head over all. Both riches and honor come from You, and You reign over all. In Your hand is power and might; Your hand it is to make great and to give strength to all.

Now let's turn to the Book of the Psalms. For starters, we have the whole chapter of Psalm 2 – Why do the nations rage, and the people plot to a vain thing? The kings of the earth set themselves and the rulers take counsel together against the Lord and against His anointing, saying "Let us break Their bonds in pieces and cast away Their cords from us." He who sits in the heavens shall laugh; the Lord shall hold them in derision. Then He shall speak to them in His wrath, and distress them in His deep displeasure: "Yet I have set My King on My holy hill of Zion. I will declare the decree: The LORD has said to Me, 'You are My Son, today I have begotten You. Ask of Me, and I will give You the nations for Your inheritance and the ends of the earth for Your possession. You shall break them with a rod of iron; You shall dash them to pieces like a potter's vessel.'" Now therefore be wise O kings; be instructed, you judges of the earth. Serve the LORD with fear and rejoice with trembling. Kiss the Son, lest He be angry, and you perish in the way, when His wrath is kindled but a little. Blessed are all those who put their trust in Him.

Moving on in the Psalms, we have Psalm 22:27-28 – All the ends of the world shall remember and turn to the LORD, and all of the families of the nations shall worship before You for the kingdom is the LORD's, and He rules over the nations. Psalm 37:23-24 – The steps of a good man are ordered by the Lord, and He delights in his way. Though he fall, he shall not be utterly cast down; for the LORD upholds him with His hand. Psalm 75:6-8 – For exaltation comes neither from the east nor from the west nor from the south. But God is the Judge: He puts down one and exalts another. For in the hand of the LORD there is a cup, and the wine is red; it is fully mixed, and

He pours it out; surely its dregs shall all the wicked of the earth drain and drink down. Psalm 95:3-5 – For the LORD is the great God, and the king above all gods. In His hands are the deep places of the earth; the heights of the hills are His also. The sea is His, for He made it; and His hands formed the dry land. Psalm 103:19 – The LORD has established His throne in heaven, and His kingdom rules over all. Psalm 115:3 – But our God is in heaven; He does whatever He pleases. Psalm 135:5-7 – For I know that the LORD is great, and our Lord is above all gods. Whatever the LORD pleases He does, in heaven and in earth, in the seas and in all deep places. He causes the vapors to ascend from the ends of the earth; He makes lightening for the rain; He brings the wind out of His treasuries.

Next, we'll turn to the Book of Daniel and see God's sovereignty in action. The pagan King Nebuchadnezzar was the most powerful king of the Chaldean dynasty of Babylonia. He had a grand kingdom. He was pompous and wanted to rule the whole world and made it known to all. But that job belongs to God alone. God chose to demonstrate His sovereignty over history and over all the nations of the earth by bringing Nebuchadnezzar to his knees in the submission to and the worship of Himself, through various incidents.

After Nebuchadnezzar besieged Jerusalem and took captives, these series of events take place. God shows His sovereignty with Daniel in the interpreting and revealing of Nebuchadnezzar's dreams. The king did not know the meaning of his first dream and wanted a wise man to not only interpret it but tell him what that dream was. But the wise men of the land knew it was humanly impossible for them to know what the king had dreamed. God delights to reveal His sovereignty in the midst of man's weaknesses and limitations though. So, enter in Daniel, who served the Most High God, the sovereign God of the universe. His God could reveal the dream and its meaning and did so.

Next, God showed His sovereignty in the fiery furnace heated up seven times more than normal after Nebuchadnezzar became enraged that three captives, Shadrach, Meshach, and Abed-Nego, would not worship his image. They proclaimed their God could deliver them, but even if He didn't, they would not bow down. They were thrown into the furnace and while the king's men who threw them in were killed from the extreme heat, God's three servants were not. As a matter of fact, the king saw four men in the furnace with the fourth appearing as the Son of God. The fire had no power over the three men and not a hair was singed, nor did even their clothing have the smell of fire.

Daniel 3:28-29 tells us what happened next. – Nebuchadnezzar spoke, saying, "Blessed be the God of Shadrach, Meshach, and Abed-Nego, who sent His Angel and delivered His servants who trusted in Him, and they have frustrated the king's word, and yielded their bodies, that they should not serve nor worship any god except their own God! Therefore, I make a decree that any people, nation, or language which speaks anything amiss against the God of Shadrach, Meshach, and Abed-Nego shall be cut in pieces, and their houses shall be made an ash heap; because there is no other God who can deliver like this."

In chapter 4, God's supreme sovereignty is displayed in fantastic fashion. Nebuchadnezzar ends up acknowledging his pride and arrogance, as well as his humbling by the sovereign hand of God. He first praises the wonders of the mighty God Most High. He then once again has a dream that no one can interpret, but Daniel. In this dream, God reveals that the king has become strong and grown to reach the heavens and his dominion to the end of the earth. Also, that God would bring it down and cause Nebuchadnezzar to be as a beast of the field until he, Nebuchadnezzar, comes to know that Heaven rules and not him. He shall eat the grass of the field wetted by the dew like an oxen does. Daniel encourages the king to break off his sins by being righteous, and his iniquities by showing mercy to the poor so that perhaps his prosperity could continue.

However, everything in the dream came upon Nebuchadnezzar a year later when he opened his mouth up wide and said, "Isn't this great Babylon that **I** have built a royal dwelling by **my** mighty power and for **my** honor as majesty?" Before he even finished speaking, a voice from heaven stated, "King Nebuchadnezzar, to you it is spoken: the kingdom has departed from you." Verse 33 says – That very hour the word was fulfilled concerning Nebuchadnezzar; he was driven from men and ate grass like oxen; his body was wet with the dew of heaven till his hair had grown like eagles' feathers and his nails like birds' claws.

We'll see what happened next in the king's own words found in Daniel 4:34-37 – And at the end of the time I, Nebuchadnezzar, lifted my eyes to heaven, and my understanding returned to me; and I blessed the Most High and praised and honored Him who lives forever: For His dominion is an everlasting dominion, and His kingdom is from generation to generation. All the inhabitants of the earth are reputed as nothing; He does according to His will in the army of heaven and among the inhabitants of the earth. No one can restrain His hand or say to Him, "What have You done?" At the same time my reason returned to me, and for the glory of my kingdom, my honor and splendor returned to me. My counselors and nobles resorted to me, I was restored to my kingdom, and excellent majesty was added to me. Now I, Nebuchadnezzar, praise and extol and honor the King of heaven, and all whose works are truth, and His ways justice. And those who walk in pride He is able to put down.

Thank you, Father! Blessed be Your Holy name! Now that we have learned of God's sovereignty over absolutely everything, and of His power to keep us in Him, He wants us to understand that everything from beginning to end, and from Genesis through Revelation, is all about Jesus.

CHAPTER THREE

JESUS IS THE THEME OF THE OLD TESTAMENT

God wants us to understand that the Old Testament is all about Jesus. It points to Jesus as our coming Messiah, and as a matter of fact, is God's narrative of redemption for the whole world. We could say that Jesus is the center, the heart, the focus, the spotlight, the theme of the entire Old Testament. Jesus Himself even tells us this in Matthew 5:17-18 – "Do not think that I came to destroy the Law or the Prophets. I did not come to destroy, but to fulfill. For assuredly I say to you, till heaven and earth pass away, one jot or one tittle will by no means pass from the law till all is fulfilled." And Jesus said in John 5:39 – "You search the Scriptures, for in them you think you have eternal life; and these are they which testify of Me." And again in John 5:46 – "For if you believed Moses, you would believe Me; for he wrote about Me."

Now let's look at Luke chapter 24, verses 27, 31-32, and 44. Verse 27 says – And beginning at Moses and all the Prophets, He expounded to them in all the Scriptures the things concerning Himself. And verses 31 and 32 say – Then their eyes were opened, and they knew Him; and He vanished. And they said to one another, "Did not our heart burn within us while He talked with us on the road, and while He opened the Scriptures to us?" Now let's jump to verse 44. It says – Then He (Jesus) said to them, "These are the words which I spoke to you while I was still with you, that all things must be fulfilled which were written in the Law of Moses and the Prophets and the Psalms concerning Me."

The Old Testament is full of types and foreshadowing of Jesus and can be found all throughout it in every Book. Many revelations of Jesus are found within the Books, but we'll focus on just one or two from each Book.

In Genesis, Jesus is the seed of woman who will crush the head of the serpent. Genesis 3:15 – And I will put enmity between you and the woman, and between your seed and her Seed; He shall bruise your head and you shall bruise His heel.

In Exodus, Jesus is foreshadowed as the Passover Lamb of God without blemish. This is unveiled within the whole 12th chapter of Exodus.

In Leviticus, Jesus is typified as our High Priest within the duties of the priests. But also, in Chapter 16, Jesus is both goats. He died as our sin offering for the forgiveness of our sins and as He accepted our sins upon Himself, He became our scapegoat. Leviticus 16:5 – "And he shall take from the congregation of the children of Israel two kids of the goats as a sin offering…" 16:8-10 – "Then Aaron shall cast lots for the two goats: one for the lot for the LORD and the other lot for the scapegoat. And Aaron shall bring the goat on which the LORD's lot fell and offer it as a sin offering. But the goat on which the lot fell to be the scapegoat shall be presented alive before the LORD, to make atonement upon it, and to let it go into the wilderness. 16:21-22 – Aaron shall lay both his hands on the head of the goat, confess over it all the iniquities of the children of Israel, and all their transgressions, concerning all their sins, putting them on the head of the goat, and shall send it away into the wilderness by the hand of a suitable man. The goat shall bear on itself all their iniquities to an uninhabited land; and he shall release the goat into the wilderness.

In Numbers, Jesus is foreshadowed as the one who is lifted up in the wilderness of sin. Numbers 21:8-9 – Then the LORD said to Moses, "Make a fiery serpent, and set it on a pole; and it shall be that everyone who is bitten, when he looks at it, shall live." So Moses made a bronze serpent, and put it on a pole; and so it was, if a serpent had bitten anyone, when he looked at the bronze serpent, he lived.

In Deuteronomy, Jesus is the prophet like Moses. Deuteronomy 18:15-19 – "The Lord your God will raise up for you a Prophet like me from your midst, from your brethren. Him you shall hear, according to all you desired of the LORD your God in Horeb in the day of assembly, saying, 'Let me not hear again the voice of the LORD my God, nor let me see this great fire anymore, lest I die.' And the Lord said to me: 'What they have spoken is good. I will raise up for them a Prophet like you from among their brethren, and will put My words in His mouth, and He shall speak to them all that I command Him. And it shall be that whoever will not hear My words, which He speaks in My name, I will require it of him.'"

In Joshua, Jesus is typified as the captain of our salvation, the one who gives us rest and leads us to the Promised Land, as found in the first chapter of Joshua as God commissioned him.

In Judges, Jesus is typified as God's appointed judge, lawgiver, and deliverer throughout the whole book, as Jesus is the True Judge of both the dead and the living.

In Ruth, Jesus is foreshadowed as Boaz, our kinsman redeemer. Ruth 2:1 – There was a relative of Naomi's husband, a man of great wealth, of the family of Elimelech. His name was Boaz. Chapter 4:1-12 – Now Boaz went up to the gate and sat down there; and behold, the close relative of whom Boaz had spoken came by. So Boaz said, "Come aside, friend, sit down here," So he came aside and sat down. And he took ten men of the elders to the city and said, "Sit down here." So, they sat down. Then he said to the close relative, "Naomi, who has come back from the country of Moab, sold the piece of land which belonged to our brother Elimelech. And I thought to inform you, saying, 'Buy it back in the presence of the inhabitants and the elders of my people. If you will redeem it, redeem it; but if you will not redeem it, then tell me, that I may know; for there is no one but you to redeem it, and I am next after you.'" And he said, "I will redeem it." Then Boaz said, "On the day you buy the field from the hand of Naomi, you must also buy it from

Ruth the Moabitess, the wife of the dead to perpetuate the name of the dead through his inheritance." And the close relative said, "I cannot redeem it for myself, lest I ruin my own inheritance. You redeem my right of redemption for yourself, for I cannot redeem it."

Now this was the custom in former times in Israel concerning redeeming and exchanging, to confirm anything: one man took off his sandal and gave it to the other, and this was a confirmation in Israel. Therefore, the close relative said to Boaz, "Buy it for yourself" So he took off his sandal. And Boaz said to the elders and all the people, "You are witnesses this day that I have bought all that was Elimelech's, and all that was Chilion's and Mahlon's, from the hand of Naomi. Moreover, Ruth the Moabitess, the widow of Mahlon, I have acquired as my wife, to perpetuate the name of the dead through his inheritance, that the name of the dead may not be cut off from among his brethren and from his position at the gate. You are witnesses this day."

And all the people who were at the gate, and the elders, said, "We are witnesses. The LORD make the woman who is coming to your house like Rachel and Leah, the two who built the house of Israel; and may you prosper in Ephrathah and be famous in Bethlehem. May your house be like the house of Perez, whom Tamar bore to Judah, because of the offspring which the LORD will give you from this young woman."

In 1 Samuel, Jesus is God rejected as the king. 1 Samuel 8:7 – And the Lord said to Samuel, "Heed the voice of the people in all that they say to you; for they have not rejected you, but they have rejected Me, that I should not reign over them."

In 2 Samuel, Jesus is the heir of David's throne and the Rock that spoke by David. 2 Samuel 5:4 – David was thirty years old when he began to reign, and he reigned forty years. Chapter 23:2-4 – "The Spirit of the LORD spoke by me, and His word was on my tongue. The God of Israel said, "The Rock of Israel spoke to me: 'He who rules over men must be just, ruling in fear of God. And he shall be like the light of the morning when the sun rises, a morning without clouds, like tender grass springing out of earth, by clear shining after rain'"

In 1 Kings, Jesus is typified as the Reigning King, and is the one who is greater than King Solomon as He states in Matthew 24:42 – "The queen of the South will rise up in judgment with this generation and condemn it, for she came from the ends of the earth to hear the wisdom of Solomon; and indeed, a greater than Solomon is here."

In 2 Kings, Jesus is foreshadowed by the prophet Elisha in the miracles performed such as multiplying bread as performed in 2 Kings 4:42-44 – Then a man came from Baal Shalisha, and brought the man of God (Elisha) bread of the first fruits, twenty loaves of barley bread, and newly ripened grain in his knapsack. And he said, "Give it to the people, that they may eat." But his servant said, "What? Shall I set this before one hundred men?" He said again, "Give it to the people, that they may eat; for thus says the LORD: 'They shall eat and have some left over.'" So, he set it before them; and they ate and had some left over, according to the word of the LORD. Jesus did and said the same thing in John 6:1-14.

In 1 Chronicles, Jesus is the son of David who is chronicled in this book. See, David was the king after God's own heart, he was the obedient king. Jesus is the obedient King unto death for the forgiveness of our sins. Jesus is the promised Messiah, meaning He had to be of the lineage of David. Matthew chapter 1 gives the genealogical proof that Jesus, in His human form, was a direct descendant of Abraham and David through Joseph, Jesus' legal father. And the genealogy in Luke chapter 3 traces Jesus' lineage through His mother, Mary. Jesus is a descendant of David by adoption through Joseph and by bloodline through Mary. This is important to understand because Jesus says in Revelation 22:16, "I am the Root and the Offspring of David," meaning, He is both the

Creator of David and the Descendant of David. Only Jesus can say this because only the Son of God made flesh can declare it.

In 2 Chronicles, Jesus is typified as the Wisdom of Solomon. Chapter 9, verse 22 – So King Solomon surpassed all the kings of the earth in riches and wisdom. 1 Kings 4:29-31 says – "And God gave Solomon, wisdom and exceedingly great understanding, and largeness of heart like the sand on the seashore. Thus, Solomon's wisdom excelled the wisdom of all the men of the East and all the wisdom of Egypt. For He was wiser than all men…" Now let's look at what Colossians 2:2-3 says about Jesus, our King of kings. – …to the knowledge of the mystery of God, both of the Father and of Christ, in whom are hidden all the treasures of wisdom and knowledge."

In Ezra, Jesus is typified as Zerubbabel, the rebuilder of the temple, in chapter 4. Then, John 2:19 says, – Jesus answered and said to them, "Destroy this temple, and in three days I will raise it up."

In Nehemiah, Jesus is typified as the rebuilder of the walls of salvation and as the guide of the remnant of God's people. Nehemiah 1:3 says – And they said to me, "The survivors who are left from the captivity in the province are there in great distress and reproach. The wall of Jerusalem is also broken down and its gates are burned with fire." And Nehemiah 2:5 says, – And I said to the king, "if it pleases the king, and if your servant has found favor in your sight, I ask that you send me to Judah, to the city of my fathers' tombs, that I may rebuild it."

Now let's look at what Paul says about God's remnant in Roman's 11:1-5 – I say then, has God cast away His people? Certainly not! For I also am an Israelite, of the seed of Abraham, of the tribe of Benjamin. God has not cast away His people whom He foreknew. Or do you not know what the Scripture says of Elijah, how he pleads with God against Israel, saying, "LORD they have killed Your prophets and torn down Your altars, and I alone am left, and they seek my life"? But what does God say to him? "I have reserved for Myself seven thousand men who have not bowed the knee to Baal." Even so then, at this present time there is a remnant according to the election of grace.

In Esther, Jesus is typified in Mordecai, our providential protector, in Esther 4:13-14 – ..."Do not think in your heart that you will escape in the king's palace any more than all the other Jews. For if you remain completely silent at this time, relief and deliverance will arise for the Jews from another place, but you and your father's house will perish. Yet who knows whether you have come to the kingdom for such a time as this?"

In Job, Jesus is foreshadowed in the need of a mediator, an advocate to plead our case to God. Job 9:32-33 says – "For He (God) is not a man, as I am, that I may answer Him, and that we should go to court together. Nor is there any mediator between us, who may lay his hand on us both. Now let's look at what 1 Timothy 2:5 says – For there is one God and one Mediator between God and men, the Man Christ Jesus.

Moving on, we have in the Psalms, Jesus as the one crucified, but not left in Sheol. Psalm 16:10 – For you will not leave my soul in Sheol, nor will You allow Your Holy One to see corruption.

In Proverbs, Jesus is the one from everlasting. Proverbs 8:22-23 – "The LORD possessed me at the beginning of His way, before His works of old. I have been established from everlasting, from the beginning of His way, before there was ever an earth." Now let's look at Jesus praying for Himself in John 17:5 – "And now, O Father, glorify Me together with Yourself, with the glory which I had with You before the world was."

In Ecclesiastes, Jesus again is the Judge of all, of both the good and the evil. Ecclesiastes 12:14 says – For God will bring every work into judgment, including every secret thing, whether good or evil. Now let's look at 2 Corinthians 5:10. It says – For we must all appear before the judgment seat of Christ, that each one may receive the things done in the body, according to what he has done, whether good or bad.

In the Song of Solomon, Jesus is typified throughout the whole book as the Lover and the Bridegroom's marriage to the bride, it's also the best example we have of true love. Now let's check out Revelation 9:7-8 – "Let us be glad and rejoice and give Him glory, for the marriage of the Lamb has come, and His wife has made herself ready. And to her it was granted to be arrayed in fine linen, clean and bright, for the fine linen is the righteous acts of the saints."

In Isaiah, Jesus is the virgin born, suffering servant. Isaiah 7:14 – "Therefore the Lord Himself will give you a sign: Behold the virgin shall conceive and bear a Son and shall call His name Immanuel. Isaiah 50:6 – "I gave my back to those who struck Me, and my cheeks to those who plucked out the beard; I did not hide my face from shame and spitting."

In Jeremiah, Jesus is the branch of righteousness mentioned in Jeremiah 23:5 – "Behold, the days are coming," says the LORD, "That I will raise to David a branch of righteousness; a King shall reign and prosper and execute judgment and righteousness in the earth."

In Lamentations, Jesus is the man of sorrows who weeps over Jerusalem as typified through the entire book as Jeremiah's weeping. We see this in Luke 19:41-44 – Now as He (Jesus) drew near, He saw the city and wept over it, saying, "If you had known, even you, especially in this your day, the things that make for your peace! But now they are hidden from your eyes. For the days will come upon you when your enemies will build an embankment around you and surround you and close you in on every side, and level you, and your children within you, to the ground; and they will not leave in you one stone upon another, because you did not know the time of your visitation."

In Ezekiel, Jesus is God's shepherd servant and prince. Ezekiel 34:23-24 – "I will establish one shepherd over them, and he shall feed them—My servant David. He shall feed them and be their shepherd. And I, the LORD, will be their God, and My servant David a prince among them; I, the LORD have spoken."

In Daniel, Jesus is the king over the kingdom that will never be destroyed. Daniel 2:44 – "And in the days of these kings the God of heaven will set up a kingdom which shall never be destroyed; and the kingdom shall not be left to other people; it shall break in pieces and consume all these kingdoms, and it shall stand forever."

In Hosea, Jesus is typified as the forgiving and redeeming husband of the unfaithful wife. Hosea 1:2 – When the LORD began to speak by Hosea, the LORD said to Hosea: "Go take a wife of harlotry and children of harlotry, for the land has committed great harlotry by departing from the LORD." And in Hosea chapter 3:1-5 – Then the LORD said to me, "Go again, love a woman who is loved by a lover and is committing adultery, just like the love of the LORD for the children of Israel, who took other gods and love the raisin cakes of the pagans." So, I bought her for myself for fifteen shekels of silver, and one and one-half homers of barley. And I said to her, "You shall stay with me many days; you shall not play the harlot, nor shall you have a man—so, too, will I be toward you." For the children of Israel shall abide many days without a king or prince, without sacrifice or sacred pillar, without ephod or teraphim. Afterward the children of Israel shall return and seek the LORD their God and David their king. They shall fear the LORD and His goodness in the latter days.

In Joel, Jesus is the savior of all mankind as seen in Joel 2:32 – And it shall come to pass that whoever calls on the name of the LORD shall be saved. For in Mount Zion and in Jerusalem there shall be deliverance, and as the LORD has said, among the remnant whom the LORD calls. Jesus is also the baptizer of the Holy Spirit in Joel 2:28-29 – And it shall come to pass afterward that I will pour out My Spirit on all flesh; your sons and your daughters shall prophesy, your old men shall dream dreams, your young men shall see visions. And also, on My menservants and on My maidservants I will pour out My Spirit in those days.

In Amos, Jesus is the rescuer of Judah in the entire context of the book. He is also the bearer of burdens, and as He bears all those burdens, God, at noon, would darken the day. We find this in Amos 8:9 "And it shall come to pass in that day," says the LORD GOD, "That I will make the sun go down at noon, and I will darken the earth in broad daylight." Now let's see what Matthew 27:45 says as Jesus hung on the cross – Now from the sixth hour until the ninth hour there was a darkness over all the land.

In Obadiah, Jesus is the holy deliverer of Mount Zion as Obadiah 1:17 shows – "But on Mount Zion there shall be deliverance, and there shall be holiness…"

In Jonah, Jesus is represented in the three days Jonah spent in the fish and is typified as overcoming the death of the grave. Matthew 12:40 reads – For as Jonah was three days in the belly of the great fish, so will the Son of Man be three days and three nights in the heart of the earth.

In Micah, Jesus is the everlasting blessing of Bethlehem. Micah 5:2 – "But you, Bethlehem Ephrathah, though you are little among the thousands of Judah, yet out of you shall come forth to Me the One to be Ruler in Israel, whose goings forth are from old, from everlasting."

In Nahum, Jesus is the stronghold in the day of wrath. Nahum 1:7 – The LORD is good, a stronghold in the time of trouble; and He knows those who trust Him.

In Habakkuk, Jesus is the justifier of those who live by faith and is typified in Habakkuk as our intercessor. Habakkuk 2:4 – "Behold the proud, his soul is not upright in him; but the just shall live by faith" Habakkuk 3:1 – A prayer of Habakkuk the prophet...

In Zephaniah, Jesus is the restorer of the remnant and the means in which all nations can worship, as found in Zephaniah 3:8-13.

In Haggai, Jesus is the shaker and Desire of All Nations and the temple of glory and peace. Haggai 2:6-9 – For thus says the LORD of hosts: 'Once more (it is a little while) I will shake heaven and earth, the sea and dry land; and I will shake all nations, and they shall come to the Desire of All Nations, and I will fill this temple with glory' says the LORD of hosts. 'And in this place, I will give peace,' says the LORD of hosts" Then in Luke 2:27-32, it states – So he came by the Spirit into the temple. And when the parents brought in the Child Jesus, to do for Him according to the custom of the law, he took Him up in his arms and blessed God and said, "Lord, now You are letting your servant depart in peace, according to Your word; For my eyes have seen Your salvation which you have prepared before the face of all peoples, a light to bring revelation to the Gentiles, and the glory of Your people Israel."

In Zechariah, Jesus is the one betrayed for 30 pieces of silver. Zechariah 11:12-13 – Then I said to them, "If it is agreeable to you, give me my wages; and if not, refrain." So, they weighed out for my wages thirty pieces of silver. And the LORD said to me, "Throw it to the potter" —that princely price they set on me. So, I took the thirty pieces of silver and threw them into the house of the LORD for the potter.

Now let's see Matthew 26:14-15 – Then one of the twelve, called Judas Iscariot, went to the chief priests and said, "What are you willing to give me if I deliver Him (Jesus) to you?" And they counted out to him thirty pieces of silver. Next let's look at Matthew

27:3-8 – Then Judas, His betrayer, seeing that He had been condemned, was remorseful and brought back the thirty pieces of silver to the chief priests and elders, saying, "I have sinned by betraying innocent blood." And they said, "What is that to us? You see to it." Then he threw down the pieces of silver in the temple and departed and went and hanged himself. But the chief priests took the silver pieces and said, "It is not lawful to put them into the treasury, because they are the price of blood." And they consulted together and bought with them the potter's field, to bury strangers in. Therefore, that field has been called the Field of Blood to this day."

In Malachi, Jesus is the one whose forerunner is Elijah. Malachi 4:5-6 – "Behold, I will send you Elijah the prophet before the coming of the great and dreadful day of the LORD. And He will turn the hearts of the fathers to the children, and the hearts of the children to their fathers, lest I come and strike earth with a curse." Now let's turn over to Luke 1:17 where Zacharias receives prophecies from an angel about his unborn child, known as John the Baptist. – "He will also go before Him (Jesus) in the spirit of Elijah, 'to turn the hearts of the fathers to the children,' and the disobedient to the wisdom of the just, to make ready a people prepared for the Lord."

Now that the Lord has established that Jesus is indeed in every Book of the Old Testament, the theme running all through it, the common thread of the whole thing, He wants us to see Jesus even more as He lays a solid foundation that we must completely understand before we get into 666. And that is what we'll discover through prophecies and their fulfillment in the next chapter. Thank you, Father, for Your revelation of Jesus through the Holy Spirit, and through Your Holy Word!

CHAPTER FOUR

IT'S ALL ABOUT JESUS

In this chapter, we'll explore some prophecies of Jesus given in the Old Testament and their fulfillment in the New Testament, so we can understand, undeniably, that God's Word is all about Jesus. Not every single prophecy will be brought forth in this chapter, but with the ones that are, there shouldn't be any doubt about it. It's all about Jesus! I still stand in awe of God's goodness and His greatness, and His undying love for us as He revealed these things to me for us, and of how His story for mankind is continually unfolding before us, generation after generation and hasn't stopped yet!

Let's now go find how the entire Word of God is indeed all about Jesus. Let's start with some prophecies concerning the birth of Jesus and His early childhood. Within these prophesies we learn that God not only planned Jesus' miraculous birth, but that He had already planned out His lineage, His bloodline, before time as we know it even began.

Let's start in Genesis 12:3 – The prophecy is that all the families of the nations will be blessed through Abraham's ancestry. God spoke to Abraham – "I will bless those who bless you, and I will curse him who curses you; and in you all the families of the earth will be blessed."

We locate the fulfillment of that prophecy in Acts 3:25-26 – "You are the sons of the prophets, and of the covenant which God made with our fathers, saying to Abraham, 'And in your seed all the families of the earth shall be blessed.' To you first, God, having raised up His Servant Jesus, sent Him to bless you, in turning away every one of you from your iniquities."

Next, we find the prophecy of God's covenant with Isaac's ancestors also in Genesis 17:19 – Then God said: "No, Sarah your wife shall bear you a son, and you shall call his name Isaac; I will establish My covenant with him for an everlasting covenant, and with his descendants after him."

We find the fulfillment of this prophecy in Romans 9:7-8 – Nor are they all children because they are the seed of Abraham; but "In Isaac your seed shall be called." That is those who are the children of flesh, these are not the children of God; but the children of the promise are counted as seed.

The next prophecy is that the nations would be blessed by Jacob's offspring too and is found in Genesis 28:13-14 –And behold, the LORD stood above it and said: "I am the LORD God of Abraham your father and the God of Isaac; the land on which you lie I will give to your descendants. Also, your descendants shall be as the dust of the earth; you shall spread abroad to the west and the east, to the north and the south; and in your seed all the families of the earth shall be blessed."

We discover this prophecy's fulfillment in Luke 3:34 where Jesus' genealogy is listed in verses 22 through 38. Verse 34 reads – the son of Jacob, the son of Isaac, the son of Abraham, the son of Terah, the son of Nahor,

The next prophecy is that the scepter shall come through Judah, and we find it in Genesis 49:10 – The scepter shall not depart from Judah, nor a lawgiver from between his feet, until Shiloh comes; and to Him shall be the obedience of the people.

We also find this fulfillment in Jesus' family line with Judah being a part of His genealogy listed in Luke chapter 3. It's found in verse 33 – the son of Amminadab, the son of Ram, the son of Hezron, the son of Judah,

The next prophecy of Jesus' lineage is that David's offspring will have an eternal kingdom and is found in 2 Samuel 7:12-13, where God makes a covenant with David. It reads, – "When your days are fulfilled and you rest with your fathers, I will set up your seed after you, who will come from your body, and I will establish his kingdom. He shall build a house for My name, and I will establish the throne of his kingdom forever."

We uncover this fulfillment in Matthew 1:1 – The book of the genealogy of Jesus Christ, the Son of David, the Son of Abraham:

Now that we've seen the prophecies fulfilled that revealed Jesus' lineage, we'll look at the prophecy of His miraculous birth. The prophecy is that a virgin shall give birth and He will be called Immanuel (God with us). This prophecy is found in Isaiah 7:14 – "Therefore the LORD Himself will give you a sign: Behold, the virgin shall conceive and bear a Son, and shall call His name Immanuel."

This fulfillment is found in Luke 1:30-35 – Then the angel said to her, "Do not be afraid, Mary, for you have found favor with God. And behold, you will conceive in your womb and bring forth a Son and shall call His name JESUS. He will be great and will be called the Son of the Highest; and the Lord God will give Him the throne of His father David. And He will reign over the house of Jacob forever, and of His kingdom there will be no end." Then Mary said to the angel, "How can this be, since I do not know a man?" And the angel answered and said to her, "The Holy Spirit will come upon you, and the power of the Highest will overshadow you; therefore, also, that Holy One who is to be born will be called the Son of God."

The next prophecy we'll look at is that Jesus will end up in Egypt. It is found in Hosea 11:1 and reads "When Israel was a child, I loved him, and out of Egypt I called My son."

We find the fulfillment in Matthew 2:13-15 – Now when they had departed, behold, an angel of the Lord appeared to Joseph in a dream, saying, "Arise, take the young Child and His mother, flee to Egypt, and stay there until I bring you word; for Herod will seek the young Child to destroy Him." When he arose, he took the young Child and His mother by night and departed for Egypt, and was there until the death of Herod, that it would be fulfilled which was spoken by the prophet, saying, "Out of Egypt I called My Son."

And we have, of course, the prophecy of the birth of Jesus taking place in Bethlehem, which is found in Micah 5:2 – "But you, Bethlehem Ephrathah, though you are little among the thousands of Judah, yet out of you shall come forth to Me The One to be Ruler in Israel, Whose goings forth are from of old, from everlasting."

We discover this fulfillment in Matthew 2:3-6 – When Herod the king heard this, he was troubled, and all Jerusalem with him. And when he had gathered all the chief priests and scribes of the people together, he inquired of them where the Christ was to be born. So they said to him, "In Bethlehem of Judea, for thus it is written by the prophet: 'But you Bethlehem, in the land of Judah, are not the least among the rulers of Judah; for out of you shall come a Ruler Who will shepherd my people Israel.'"

Next, in the following prophecies, we'll look at the profound ministry God planned for Jesus to have while He walked here on earth. The first one is that His ministry will destroy the devil's work and is found in Genesis 3:15 – "And I will put enmity between you and the woman, and between your seed and her Seed; He shall bruise your head, and you shall bruise His heel."

We find the confirmation of this in 1 John 3:8 – He who sins is of the devil, for the devil has sinned from the beginning. For this purpose the Son of God was manifested, that He might destroy the works of the devil.

Now let's take a look at the prophecy of Jesus having a blemish free, sinless life and ministry. We find this in Exodus 12:5 – Your lamb shall be without blemish, a male of the first year. You may take it from the sheep or from goats.

Look at what Hebrew 9:14 says to see the fulfillment. It states, how much more shall the blood of Christ, who through the eternal Spirit offered Himself without spot to God, cleanse your conscience from dead works to serve the living God?

In Psalm 8:4-6, we find the prophecy of Jesus being humbled to become a man of flesh in order to serve mankind. It reads, "What is man that you are mindful of him, and the son of man that you visit him? For you have made him a little lower than the angels, and You have crowned him with glory and honor. You have made him to have dominion over the works of Your hands; You have put all things under his feet,"

Now let's take a look at Hebrews 2:5-9 to observe the fulfillment. It says – For He has not put the world to come, of which we speak, in subjection to angels. But one testified in a certain place, saying: "What is man that you are mindful of him, and the son of man that you take care of him? You have made him a little lower than the angels; You have crowned him with glory and honor and set him over the works of Your hands. You have put all things in subjection under his feet." For in that He put all in subjection under him, He left nothing that is not put under him. But now we do not yet see all things put under him. But we see Jesus, who was made a little lower than the angels, for the suffering of death crowned with glory and honor, that He, by the grace of God, might taste death for everyone."

Psalms 40:6-8 takes us to the next prophecy, which is that Jesus would be the perfect sacrifice. It reads – Sacrifice and offering You did not desire; my ears You have opened. Burnt offering and sin offering You did not require. Then I said, "Behold, I come; in the scroll of the book it is written of me. I delight to do Your will, O my God, and Your law is within my heart."

Now let's look at the prophecy's fulfillment in Hebrews 10:5-10 – Therefore when He came into the world, He said:

"Sacrifice and offering You did not desire, but a body You have prepared for Me. In burnt offerings and sacrifices for sin You had no pleasure. Then I said, 'Behold, I have come—in the volume of the Book it is written of Me—to do Your will, O God.'" Previously saying, "Sacrifice and offering, burnt offerings, and offerings for sin You did not desire, nor had pleasure in them" (which are offered according to the law), then He said, "Behold, I have come to do Your will, O God." He takes away the first that He may establish the second. By that will we have been sanctified through the body of Jesus Christ once for all.

Another prophecy is that Jesus would preach righteousness to Israel and is found in Psalm 40:9 – I have proclaimed the good news of the righteousness in the great assembly; indeed, I do not restrain my lips, O LORD, You Yourself know.

We discover the fulfillment of this one in Matthew 4:17 – From that time Jesus began to preach and to say, "Repent, for the kingdom of heaven is at hand."

The next prophecy we'll look at is that Jesus will teach in parables and is found in Psalm 78:1-2 – Give ear, O my people, to my law; incline your ears to the words of my mouth. I will open my mouth in a parable; I will utter dark sayings of old,

The fulfillment to this one is found in Matthew 13:34-35 – All of these things Jesus spoke to the multitude in parables; and without a parable He did not speak to them, that it might be fulfilled which was spoken by the prophet, saying: "I will open My mouth in parables; I will utter things kept secret from the foundation of the world."

Another prophecy is that Jesus' parables would fall on deaf ears in Isaiah 6:9-10 – And He said, "Go and tell this people: 'Keep on hearing, but do not understand; keep on seeing, but do not perceive.' Make the heart of this people dull, and their ears heavy, and shut their eyes; lest they see with their eyes, and hear with their ears, and understand with their heart, and return and be healed.'"

Matthew 13:13-15 shows the fulfillment. It reads, "Therefore I speak to them in parables, because seeing they do not see, and hearing they do not hear, nor do they understand. And in them the prophecy of Isaiah is fulfilled, which says: 'Hearing you will hear and shall not understand and seeing you will see and not perceive; for the hearts of this people have grown dull. Their ears are hard of hearing, and their eyes they have closed, lest they should see with their eyes and hear with their ears, lest they should understand with their hearts and turn, so that I should heal them.'"

The next prophecy we'll look at is that Jesus would be a stone that causes people to stumble. It's found in Isaiah 8:14 – He will be a sanctuary, but a stone of stumbling and a rock of offense to both the houses of Israel, as a trap and a snare to the inhabitants of Jerusalem.

We'll turn to 1 Peter 2:7-8 to see the fulfillment. It reads, Therefore, to you who believe, He is precious; but to those who are disobedient, "The stone which the builders rejected has become the chief cornerstone", and "A stone of stumbling and a rock of offense." They stumble, being disobedient to the word, to which they were also appointed.

The next prophecy we'll discuss is that Jesus' ministry would begin in Galilee and is found in Isaiah 9:1-2 – Nevertheless the gloom will not be upon her who is distressed, as when at first, He lightly esteemed the land of Zebulun and the land of Naphtali, and afterward more heavily oppressed her, by the way of the sea, beyond the Jordon, in Galilee of the Gentiles. The people who walked in darkness have seen a great light; those who dwelt in the land of the shadow of death, upon them a light has shined.

We discover this fulfillment in Matthew 4:12-17 – Now when Jesus heard that John had been put in prison, He departed to

Galilee. And leaving Nazareth, He came and dwelt in Capernaum, which is by the sea, in the regions of Zebulun and Naphtali, that it might be fulfilled which was spoken by Isaiah the prophet, saying: "The land of Zebulun and the land of Naphtali, by the way of the sea, beyond the Jordon, Galilee of the Gentiles; the people who sat in darkness have seen a great light, and upon those who sat in the region and shadow of death Light has dawned." From that time Jesus began to preach and to say, "Repent, for the kingdom of heaven is at hand."

In Isaiah 11:10, we find the next prophecy of Jesus' ministry declaring that Jesus would draw the Gentiles to Himself. It says, "And in that day there shall be a Root of Jesse, who shall stand as a banner to the people; for the Gentiles shall seek Him, and His resting place shall be glorious."

Now let's read the fulfillment in John 12:18-21 – For this reason the people also met Him, because they heard that He had done this sign. The Pharisees therefore said among themselves, "You see that you are accomplishing nothing. Look, the world has gone after Him!" Now there were certain Greeks among those who came up to worship at the feast. Then they came to Philip, who was from Bethsaida of Galilee, and asked him, saying, "Sir, we wish to see Jesus."

Next, we'll look at the prophecy of Jesus having a ministry of miracles. It's located in Isaiah 35:5-6 – Then the eyes of the blind shall be opened, and the ears of the deaf shall be unstopped. Then the lame shall leap like a deer, and the tongue of the dumb to sing. For waters shall burst forth in the wilderness, and streams in the desert.

This prophecy is recorded as coming to pass in Matthew 11:2-6 – And when John had heard in prison about the works of Christ, he sent two of his disciples and said to Him, "Are You the coming One, or do we look for another?" Jesus answered and said to them, "Go tell John the things which you hear and see: "The blind see and the lame walk; the lepers are cleansed and the deaf hear; the dead are raised up and the poor have the gospel preached to them. "And blessed is he who is not offended because of Me."

The next prophecy is that Jesus would have a forerunner and is found In Isaiah 40:3 – The voice of one crying in the wilderness: "Prepare the way of the LORD; make straight in the desert a highway for our God." In John 1:23, we find the fulfillment – "He (John the Baptist) said: "I am 'The voice of one crying in the wilderness: Make straight the way of the LORD,'" as the prophet Isaiah said."

Continuing on, we find Jesus prophesied of as being a mild and tender redeemer of the Gentiles in Isaiah 42:1-4 – "Behold! My Servant whom I uphold, My Elect One in whom My soul delights! I have put My Spirit upon Him; He will bring forth justice to the Gentiles. He will not cry out, nor raise His voice, nor cause His voice to be heard in the street. A bruised reed He will not break, and smoking flax He will not quench; He will bring forth justice for truth. He will not fail nor be discouraged, till He has established justice in the earth; and the coastlands shall wait for His law."

Now look what we find in Matthew 12:15-21 – But when Jesus knew it, He withdrew from there. And great multitudes followed Him, and He healed them all. Yet He warned them not to make Him known, that it might be fulfilled which was spoken by Isaiah the prophet saying: "Behold! My servant whom I have chosen, My Beloved in whom My soul is well pleased! I will put My Spirit upon Him, and He will declare justice to the Gentiles. He will not quarrel nor cry out, nor will anyone hear His voice in the streets. A bruised reed He will not break, and smoking flax He will not quench till He sends forth justice to victory; and in His name Gentiles will trust."

There are many more prophesies of Jesus fulfilled as well, too many to include them all, but I want to share one of my favorites before we move on to the next set. We find the prophecy of Jesus' resurrection in Job 19:23-27 – "Oh that my words were written! Oh, that they were inscribed in a book! That they were engraved on a rock with an iron pen and lead, forever! For I know that my Redeemer lives, and He shall stand at the last on the earth; and after my skin is destroyed, this I know, that in my flesh I shall see God, whom I shall see for myself, and my eyes shall behold, and not another. How my heart yearns within me!"

We see fulfillment in John 5:24-29 – "Most assuredly, I say to you, he who hears My word and believes in Him who sent Me has everlasting life, and shall not come into judgment, but has passed from death to life. Most assuredly, I say to you, the hour is coming, and now is, when the dead will hear the voice of the Son of God; and those who hear will live. For as the Father has life in Himself, and has given Him authority to execute judgment also, because He is the Son of Man. Do not marvel at this; for the hour is coming in which all who are in the graves will hear His voice and come forth—those who have done good, to the resurrection of life, and those who have done evil, to the resurrection of condemnation."

As I previously stated, there are many more prophecies about Jesus throughout the Old Testament fulfilled in the New, but to bring home how awesome God and His Word are concerning His Son Jesus, we'll now focus on over two dozen prophecies regarding Him, all spoken at least 500 years before, that all came to pass in just one day! Our God is truly an awesome God!

Jesus will betrayed by a friend found in Psalm 41:9 – Even my own familiar friend in whom I trusted, who ate my bread, has lifted up his heel against me. And Matthew 26:49 –Immediately he (Judas) went up to Jesus and said, "Greetings, Rabbi!" and kissed Him.

The price of Jesus' betrayal will be 30 pieces of silver in Zechariah 11:12 – Then I said to them, "If it is agreeable to you, give me my wages; and if not, refrain." So, they weighed out for my wages thirty pieces of silver. And Matthew 26:14-15 – Then one of the twelve, called Judas Iscariot, went to the chief priests and said, "What are you willing to give me if I deliver Him to you?" And they counted out to him thirty pieces of silver.

His betrayal money will be cast to the floor of my temple in Zechariah 11:13 – And the LORD said to me, "Throw it to the potter" —that princely price they set on me. So, I took the thirty pieces of silver and threw them into the house of the LORD for the potter. And Matthew 27:5 – Then he threw down the pieces of silver into the temple and departed and went out and hanged himself.

His betrayal money will be used to buy the potter's field in Zechariah 11:13 (see above) and Matthew 27:7 – And they consulted together and bought with them the potter's field, to bury strangers in."

Jesus will be forsaken and deserted by His disciples in Zechariah 13:7 – "Awake, O sword, against My Shepherd, against the Man who is My companion," Says the LORD of hosts. "Strike the Shepherd, and the sheep will be scattered…" And Mark 14:50 – Then they all forsook Him and fled.

Jesus will be accused by false witnesses in Psalm 35:11 – "Fierce witnesses rise up; they ask me things that I do not know". And Matthew 26:59-60 – Now the chief priests, the elders, and all the council sought false testimony against Jesus to put Him to death but found none. Even though many false witnesses came forward, they found none. But at last, two false witnesses came forward.

Jesus will be silent before His accusers in Isaiah 53:7 – He was oppressed, and He was afflicted, yet He opened not His mouth; He was led as a lamb to the slaughter, and as a sheep before its shearers is silent, so He opened not His mouth. And in Matthew

27:12 – And while He was being accused by the chief priests and elders, He answered nothing.

Jesus will be wounded and bruised in Isaiah 53:5 – But He was wounded for our transgressions, He was bruised for our iniquities… And Matthew 27:26 – Then he released Barabbas to them; and when he had scourged Jesus, he delivered Him to be crucified.

Jesus will be hated without a cause in Psalm 69:4 – Those who hate Me without a cause are more than the hairs of My head… And in John 15:25 – "But this happened that the word might be fulfilled which is written in their law, 'They hated Me without a cause.'"

Jesus will be struck and spit upon in Isaiah 50:6 – I gave My back to those that struck Me, and my cheeks to those who plucked out the beard; I did not hide My face from shame and spitting. And Matthew 26:67 – Then they spat in His face and beat Him; and others struck Him with the palms of their hands,

Jesus will be mocked, ridiculed and rejected in Isaiah 53:3 – He is despised and rejected by men, a Man of sorrows and acquainted with grief. And we hid, as it were, our faces from Him; He was despised, and we did not esteem Him. And Matthew 27:27-31 – Then the soldiers of the governor took Jesus into the Praetorium and gathered the whole garrison around Him, and they stripped Him and put a scarlet robe on Him. When they had twisted a crown of thorns, they put it on His head, and a reed in His right hand. And they bowed the knee before Him and mocked Him, saying, "Hail, King of the Jews!", and John 7:5, 48 – For even His brothers did not believe Him… "Have any of the rulers or the Pharisees believed in Him?"

Jesus will collapse from weakness in Psalm 109:24 – My knees are weak through fasting, and my flesh is feeble from lack of fatness. I also have become a reproach to them; when they look at me, they shake their heads. And we find this in Luke 23:26 – Now as they led Him away, they laid hold of Simon a Cyrenian, who was coming from the country, and on him they laid the cross that he might bear it after Jesus.

Jesus will be taunted with specific words and people will shake their heads at Him – Psalm 22:6-8 – But I am a worm, and no man; a reproach of men, and despised by the people. All those who see Me ridicule Me; they shoot out the lip, they shake the head saying, "He trusted in the LORD, let Him rescue Him; Let Him deliver Him; since He delights in Him". And Psalm 109:25 – I also have become a reproach to them; when they look at me, they shake their heads. We find this in Matthew 27:39-43 – And those who passed by blasphemed Him, wagging their heads and saying, "You who destroy the temple and build it in three days, save Yourself! If You are the Son of God, come down from the cross." Likewise, the chief priests also, mocking with the scribes and elders said, "He saved others; Himself He cannot save. If He is the King of Israel, let Him come down from the cross, and we will believe Him; for He said, 'I am the Son of God.'"

People will stare at Jesus found in Psalm 22:17 – I can count all my bones. They look and stare at Me. We discover this in Luke 23:35 – And the people stood looking on. But even the rulers with them sneered, saying, "He saved others; let Him save Himself if He is the Christ, the chosen of God."

Jesus will be executed among 'sinners' prophesied in Isaiah 53:12 – Therefore I will divide Him a portion with the great, and He shall divide the spoil with the strong, because He poured out His soul unto death, and He was numbered with the transgressors, and He bore the sin of many, and made intercession for the transgressors. We locate the fulfillment of this in Matthew 27:38 – Then two robbers were crucified with Him, one on the right and another on the left.

Jesus' hands and feet will be pierced found in Psalm 22:16 – For dogs have surrounded Me; the congregation of the wicked has enclosed Me. They pierced My hands and My feet. And we see this come to pass in combination of Luke 23:33 – And when they had come to the place called Calvary, there they crucified Him...and Luke 24:39 – "Behold My hands and My feet, that it is I Myself..."

Jesus will pray for His persecutors as found in Isaiah 53:12 – Therefore I will divide Him a portion with the great, and He shall divide the spoil with the strong, because He poured out His soul unto death, and He was numbered with the transgressors, and He bore the sin of many, and made intercession for the transgressors. We find Jesus praying for the transgressors in Luke 23:34 – Then Jesus said, "Father, forgive them, for they do not know what they do."

Jesus' family will stand afar off and watch found in Psalm 38:11 – My loved ones and my friends stand aloof from my plague, and my relatives stand afar off. We see this come to pass in Luke 23:49 – But all His acquaintances, and the women who followed Him, stood a distance, watching these things.

Jesus' garments will be divided up and divvied out by the casting of lots found in Psalm 22:18 – They divide my garments among them, and for my clothing they cast lots. We find this come to pass in John 19:23-24 – Then the soldiers, when they had crucified Jesus, took His garments and made four parts, to each soldier a part, and also the tunic. Now the tunic was without seam, woven from the top in one piece. They said therefore among themselves, "Let us not tear it, but cast lots for it, whose it shall be," that the Scripture might be fulfilled which says: "They divided My garments among them, and for My clothing they cast lots." Therefore the soldiers did these things.

Jesus will thirst and is seen in Psalm 69:21 – They also gave Me gall for My food, and for my thirst they gave Me vinegar to drink. John 19:28 says, After this, Jesus knowing that all things were now accomplished, that the Scripture might be fulfilled, said, "I thirst!" And Matthew 27:34 says they gave Him sour wine mingled with gall to drink. But when He had tasted it, He would not drink.

Jesus will commit Himself to God as stated in Psalm 31:5 – Into your hand I commit my spirit; You have redeemed me, O LORD God of truth. And this is fulfilled in Luke 23:46 – And when Jesus had cried out with a loud voice, He said, "Father, 'into Your hands I commit My Spirit.'"

Jesus' bones will be left unbroken is found in Psalm 34:20 – He guards all his bones; not one of them is broken. And we find this fulfillment in John 19:33 – But when they came to Jesus and saw that He was already dead, they did not break His bones.

Jesus' side will be pierced is found in Zechariah 12:10 – "And I will pour on the house of David and on the inhabitants of Jerusalem the Spirit of grace and supplication; then they will look on Me whom they pierced. Yes, they will mourn for Him as one mourns for his only son, and grieve for Him as one grieves for a firstborn." In John 19:34, we find the fulfillment. It reads, But one of the soldiers pierced His side with a spear, and immediately blood and water came out.

It was prophesied that darkness would come over the land at midday in Amos 8:9 – "And it shall come to pass in that day," says the Lord God, "That I will make the sun go down at noon, and I will darken the earth in broad daylight." Now let's look at Matthew 27:45 – Now from the sixth hour until the ninth hour there was darkness over all the land.

And lastly, Jesus would be buried in a rich man's tomb found in Isaiah 53:9 – And they made His grave with the wicked—but with the rich at His death, because He had done no violence, nor was any deceit in His mouth. We see this come to pass in Matthew 27:57-60 – Now when evening had come, there came a rich man from Arimathea, named Joseph, who himself had also become a disciple of Jesus. This man went to Pilate and asked for the body of Jesus. Then Pilate commanded the body to be given to him. When Joseph had taken the body, he wrapped it in a clean linen cloth, and laid it in his new tomb which he had hewn out of the rock; and he rolled a large stone against the door of the tomb and departed.

Right there, we have over two dozen prophecies all fulfilled in one day, a 24-hour period, prophecies spoken hundreds of years before these events took place! Hallelujah! Praise Father God! But you know what? There is no way I am going to leave Jesus in the grave. God didn't and neither will I!

So, as a final testimony, on the third day after His death, Jesus will be raised from the dead. Psalm 16:10 says, For you will not leave my soul in Sheol, nor will You allow Your Holy One to see corruption. And Acts 2:31 shows us the fulfillment. It reads, "he, foreseeing this, spoke concerning the resurrection of the Christ, that His soul was not left in Hades, nor did His flesh see corruption."

And Jesus will ascend to heaven found in Psalm 68:18 – You have ascended on high. You have led captivity captive; You have received gifts among men, even from the rebellious, that the LORD God might dwell there." Now look at Acts 1:9 – Now when He had spoken these things, while they watched, He was taken up, and a cloud received Him out of their sight.

As well as Jesus will be seated at the right hand of God in full majesty and authority. Psalm 110:1 prophesies The LORD said to my Lord, "Sit at My right hand, till I make Your enemies Your footstool." And we find this fulfillment spoken of in Hebrews 1:3 – who being the brightness of His glory and the express image of His person and upholding all things by the word of His power, when He had purged our sins, sat down at the right hand of the Majesty on high.

As these prophecies reveal, God planned our salvation all the way back before the Garden of Eden. Jesus' life, death and resurrection are the most important events to ever take place in all of history. Therefore, it should be no surprise to see that God would give us all these signs of His plans throughout Israel's history and through the prophets. Jesus' story reveals God's incredible love for us and through it, we learn how incredibly thorough His plan for redeeming us is. Because of Jesus, we can all be reconciled to Father God through Jesus' sacrifice and resurrection! This is why it's all about Jesus!

CHAPTER FIVE

A REVELATION OF REVELATION

Now that God has laid out the foundation He wanted set, with us knowing He had a plan before He even laid out the foundation of the world, and that He has complete and total sovereignty over absolutely everything, and that His plan is all about Jesus, we can now begin to unravel with wisdom and understanding, the number 666 as found in the Book of Revelation.

One of the times I was in prayer regarding this book, asking the Lord to show me what He wanted written, I heard the Holy Spirit ask me, "If you were to ask random people what they thought the Book of Revelation was about, what do you think they would answer you?" I replied that the answer I would surely get would be that it's about the end times or last days. Then the Lord told me to turn to the first chapter of Revelation and read the first phrase in the first sentence. I opened my Bible and turned to Revelation 1:1 and began to read. – The Revelation of Jesus Christ…

Then He asked me to go to the very top of the page and read what it said. The complete title of the Book of Revelation at the top of the page in my Bible reads, THE REVELATION OF JESUS CHRIST. Wow! We are told right from the start that the Book of Revelation is the revealing of Jesus by Jesus, which God gave Him to reveal to His servants. The entire book is all about Jesus, who Jesus was, is and always will be. It's about Jesus' entire life! I understood there was a great disconnect between what the book was really about and what has been taught about it for years. The Lord gave me the understanding that Revelation is not just Jesus revealing to John what would happen in the future, but is an ongoing revelation of Jesus Himself, and all that entails! It's Jesus as The Alpha and Omega, the Beginning and the End, just like Jesus says He is!

Next, the Holy Spirit brought my attention to the word Revelation in the first sentence of Revelation 1:1. It was then I noticed that it has a capital "R". All other Scripture using the word revelation use the lower case "r". As examples, let's look at Romans 16:25 – Now to Him who is able to establish you according to my gospel and the preaching of Jesus Christ, according to the *revelation* of the mystery kept secret since the world began. And at Galatians 1:12 – For I neither received it from man, nor was I taught it, but it came through the *revelation* of Jesus Christ.

As I read these Scriptures, I also realized that everything written in reference to God, the Holy Spirit and Jesus, is always capitalized. Scripture is capitalized because it is Jesus as Revelation 19:13 and 16 say – He was clothed with a robe dipped in blood, and His name is called The Word of God…And He has on His robe and on His thigh a name written: KING OF KINGS AND LORD OF LORDS. All words referencing Jesus are capitalized whether it be He, His, You, Your, etc. So, the "Revelation" is Jesus.

Once again, Father God is showing us that the entire Word of God is all about Jesus. All of it! And if He is showing us in so many various ways, then we need to understand that it is of utmost importance. So, to briefly recap, we could say that Jesus is foretold, typified, and prophesied about throughout the Old Testament. He's made known in the flesh throughout the Gospels. Jesus is preached and testified about throughout the Acts. He's expounded upon throughout the Epistles, and He's revealed throughout Revelation. Truly, it is all about Jesus! Thank you, Father!

As I thought back on what people would answer regarding the question of what the Book of Revelation is about, my curiosity was roused about the end times as I've been reading about them and the last days in a slew of Scriptures throughout the New Testament for absolutely years. So, I went back to read them with a different frame of mind. Let's take a look at some of these Scripture verses to further help our understanding.

Acts 2:16-18 – "But this is what was spoken by the prophet Joel: 'And it shall come to pass in the *last days*, says God, that I will pour out my Spirit on all flesh; your sons and your daughters shall prophecy, your young men shall see visions, your old men shall dream dreams. And I will pour out my Spirit in those days; and they shall prophesy.'"

Hebrews 1:1-2 – God, who at various times and in various ways spoke in time past to the fathers by the prophets, has in these *last days* spoken to us by His Son, whom He has appointed heir of all things, through whom also made the worlds…

1 Timothy 4:1-2 – Now the Spirit expressly says that in *latter times* some will depart from the faith, giving heed to deceiving spirits and doctrines of demons, speaking lies in hypocrisy, having their own conscience seared with a hot iron…

1 Peter 1:18-20 – Knowing that you were not redeemed with corruptible things, like silver and gold, from your aimless conduct received by tradition from your fathers, but with the precious blood of Christ, as a lamb without blemish and without spot. He indeed was foreordained before the foundation of the world but was manifest in these *last times* for you.

1 John 2:18 – Little children, it is the *last hour*; and as you have heard that the Antichrist is coming, even now many antichrists have come, by which we know that it is the *last hour*.

    Do you see that? The last days began with Jesus' birth, death, resurrection, and ascension into heaven, and this was taught and preached throughout the Acts and Epistles. Now we can understand why people have been saying it is the last days for generations— because it is! However, that should not be a reason for people to be blasé about it and blow off salvation or for those who are saved to just play with the things of God, not being a faithful servant sold out to Jesus, giving Him their all, being just lukewarm as opposed to being on fire for Him, citing they have time. Jesus addressed this in

Matthew 24:42-44 – "Watch therefore, for you do not know what hour your Lord is coming. But know this, that if the master of the house had known what hour the thief would come, he would have watched and not allowed his house to be broken into. Therefore, you also be ready, for the Son of Man is coming at an hour you do not expect." And in Revelation 3:15-16, Jesus says – "I know your works, that you are neither cold nor hot. I could wish you were cold or hot. So then, because you are lukewarm, and neither cold nor hot, I will vomit you out of my mouth." There is a flip side to this as well.

The Lord asked me, "Why do you suppose men put Me on a timetable? Do they not know that My timing is different than the timing of men? Does not My Word say to not forget this one thing, that with Me, one day is as a thousand years and a thousand years as one day? Do they not know that a thousand years is a millennium in their time but may or may not be in Mine? Do they not know that I cannot be put into a timetable box and that I refuse to fit into a man-made box of any kind? Do they not know that it is a scheme of the enemy, a scheme of the god of this age, to take advantage of the traditions of men, to have wicked men devise dubious plots that sound like they come out of the timetable that men have made from the Book of Revelation, to inflict fear into the hearts of men, women, and children without understanding? And that they do so for their own diabolical agendas? This is why we are in a season of shining the light of My Word on the darkness of the traditions of men", says the Lord of hosts.

We must understand that God is outside of our time and is indeed the One who created time. He is eternal and so any attempt by any man or mankind to put Him on a timetable is just silly and shows a lack of understanding and wisdom. After He spoke this to me, I prayed that we all may have the same wisdom and understanding as Moses did in Psalm 90:1-6 – Lord, You have been our dwelling place in all generations. Before the mountains were brought forth, or ever You had formed the earth and the world, even from everlasting to everlasting, You are God. You turn man to destruction, and say, "Return, O children of men." For a thousand years in Your sight are like yesterday when it is past, and like a watch in the night. You carry them away like a flood; they are like a sleep. In the morning it flourishes and grows up; in the evening it is cut down and withers.

And 2 Peter 1:19-21 says – And so we have the prophetic word confirmed, which you do well to heed as a light that shines in a dark place, until the day dawns and the morning star rises in your hearts knowing this first, that no prophecy of Scripture is of any private interpretation, for prophecy never came by the will of man, but holy men of God spoke as they were moved by the Holy Spirit.

Jesus showed me how foolish the timetable of the traditions of men truly is. He reminded me that when He was discussing His return, coming in the clouds of heaven with power and glory, He told His disciples in Matthew 24:36, "But of that day and hour no one knows, not even the angels of heaven, but My Father only." He then asked me a question that made perfect sense and confirmed what the Spirit has been revealing to me, giving me confidence to continue on. Thank you Lord! Jesus asked me, "If I don't know the time of My return, nor do the angels of heaven, but only My Father, then how could I reveal it to John in a timetable?" Well, that makes total sense. If Jesus doesn't know it, then He certainly cannot share or reveal it!

The Holy Spirit showed me a word spoken by the prophet Jeremiah in my NIV version of the Bible, showing me how it is a timely word in our day regarding the customs and traditions of men being taught today. Jeremiah 10:2-3 – This is what the LORD says: Do not learn the ways of the nations or be terrified by signs in the sky, though the nations are terrified by them. For the customs of the peoples are worthless… Once again, God is showing us that the traditions of men being taught are as worthless today as they were way back then as they come from the minds of men and not from revelation given by the Holy Spirit of God. And just like back in Jeremiah's time, fear was inflicted on peoples by "signs". We should not fear because of the customs and traditions of men pointing to goings on around us as signs since their traditions and customs are worthless! John tells us in John 3:31 – "He who comes from above is above all; he who is of the earth is earthly and speaks of the earth. He who comes from heaven is above all." Thank You Father God!

I hear the Spirit of the Lord saying that we need to recognize the traditions of men more than ever before, and dispose of them properly, making room for the Holy Spirit to fill us with more and more of Him, for we are entering a season where God will be turning the focus of the world on His people more and more. Thank you Father! Thank you Jesus! Hallelujah! Lead us by Your Spirit to do a check within our own, so that we may give more and more of ourselves to You, so that we may think, look and act more and more like You in every aspect of our lives, that our light (Jesus) may shine brighter and brighter as the world around us catapults into darkness more and more! Hallelujah!

Now let's turn to the Scripture in Revelation pertaining to 666. Revelation 13:16-18 – He causes all, both small and great, rich and poor, free and slave, to receive a mark on their right hand or on their foreheads, and that no one may buy or sell except one who has the mark or the name of the beast, or the number of his name. Here is wisdom. Let him who has understanding calculate the number of the beast, for it is the number of a man: His number is 666.

In Revelation 13:18, we discover the number of the beast is the same as the number of a man in general or mankind or all humanity. "Here is wisdom. Let him who has understanding calculate the number of the beast, for it is the number of a man: His number is 666." When the Lord showed me this, I began to pray and seek Him as what He wanted me to know from this verse. I was thinking that throughout times, different people have stated who they believed or thought the beast was from this Scripture partnered with

Revelation 13:3, 12. Verse 3 says, And I saw one of his heads as if it had been mortally wounded, and his deadly wound was healed. And all the world marveled and followed the beast. Verse 12 states, And he exercises all the authority of the first beast in his presence, and causes the earth and those who dwell in it to worship the first beast, whose deadly wound was healed.

I remembered once reading someone thought the antichrist would be Hitler brought back to life because his face is one that the whole world would recognize coupled with the atrocities he committed against God's chosen people, the Jewish. I remembered reading once someone else thought it would be Nero Caesar brought back because in the Hebrew language the letters have numerical value and his equaled 666. I also remembered reading someone else thought it would be Judas Iscariot because of the son of perdition reference to both of them. It was then I heard the Lord speak to me. He asked me, "What difference does it make?" I didn't understand what He was asking so I asked Him what He meant by that question. He answered with, "What difference does it make what the name is? Figuring out a name of who it might be will not make one bit of difference. That is not what My Word is saying. My Word says wisdom and understanding is calculating the 'number' of the name and understanding that, not calculating a name by the number."

As I contemplated on the Lord's answer, I was reminded that man was created on the sixth day, so therefore the number of man was six. The text reads "a man", but some translations state "man", but either way, the number of man is six. Also, I was reminded that the number six also stands for incomplete and imperfection as being just shy of the number seven, which stands for completion and perfection. In the Bible perfection means completeness or in other words, absolute wholeness. More specifically, in the New Testament, perfection also means maturity. The Word speaks of perfection in at least three different aspects. They are the perfection of God, the perfection of Jesus, and the perfection of man or human beings.

Matthew 5:48 says, "…your Father in heaven is perfect." The Scriptures teach us that Jesus was made perfect through suffering. Hebrews 2:8-9 reads, "though He was a Son, yet He learned obedience by the things which He suffered. And having been perfected, He became the author of eternal salvation to all whom obey Him". James encourages us to reach perfection in James 1:4. "But let patience have its perfect work, that you may be perfect and complete, lacking nothing." Paul also taught that our goal is to reach for perfection, to strive to become perfected just as he did. He recognized he wasn't perfected yet but was pressing on for it in Philippians 3:12. "Not that I have already attained, or am already perfected; but I press on, that I may lay hold of that for which Christ Jesus has also laid hold of me."

So here we see that God is perfect, Jesus is perfect, but man isn't yet, although He should strive to be so, meaning we are six, less than perfect. So, we could say that 666 is man, man, man. We'll go deeper into this revelation in further detail in upcoming chapters, but in the next chapter, we'll look at other aspects of Revelation 13:16.

CHAPTER SIX

FOREHEADS AND HANDS

Revelation 13:16 – He causes all, both small and great, rich and poor, free and slave, to receive a mark on their right hand or on their foreheads.

As I prayerfully contemplated on this Scripture, the word "forehead" just jumped off the page of my Bible at me, and I heard the Spirit say He would show me the significance of the forehead and hands all through the Scriptures, both naturally and spiritually. He said He would show me how this Scripture was not just a thing of the end of time as some have supposed and therefore have taught in the church, but actually has been from the beginning and will be to the end, just like Jesus. Wow!

When I heard and thought about the word "naturally", my mind jumped back to my medical training, and I remembered learning that the cerebrum part of the brain is directly behind our foreheads and is the largest part of our brain. The cerebrum is the part of the brain that enables thinking, judgment, reasoning, and problem solving. It's where thoughts originate and what path they lead us to from there. It's the part of the brain that is responsible for our emotions and learning. Our cerebrum, therefore, is where memorization takes place, as well as where all of our higher intellectual functions occur. It's where we make choices from. And it controls all of our voluntary actions. It is what sends the signal for us to raise our hand and wave when we see somebody we know. It commands the legs and feet to move and sets the pace of how fast, according to whether we choose to run, walk, or just leisurely stroll, for example.

We could say that the cerebrum is the seat or throne for the ruler of our bodies, or in other words, is the ruler of our flesh. So then, 666 could also be said as flesh, flesh, flesh. We'll discuss the flesh in greater depth later on, but now let's take a journey through the Scriptures and learn about the significance of the forehead. Let's take a look at Exodus 28:36-38, when God was giving instructions regarding the priestly garments that Aaron, the high priest was to wear. It reads, "You shall also make a plate of pure gold and engrave on it, like the engraving of a signet: HOLINESS TO THE LORD. And you shall put it on a blue cord, that it may be on the turban; it shall be on the front of the turban. So, it shall be on Aaron's forehead, that Aaron may bear the iniquity of the holy things which the children of Israel hallow in all their holy gifts; and it shall always be on his forehead, that they may be accepted before the Lord."

What we learn here is that the chief priest had to display his allegiance to God in the most prominent place of the body, the forehead. He is displaying that he no longer is his own but belongs to God and has dedicated his life to be in service to God for the people. The golden sign HOLINESS TO THE LORD displayed on the forehead was a constant reminder to all involved that there was an agreement made between God and the man Aaron and that his life was set apart for God. In seeing this Scripture, we could say then, that our forehead is an advertisement billboard.

Now, let's see another place where God utilized a forehead for advertisement. We find this in the 26th chapter of 2 Chronicles. Here we find Uzziah was made king in Judah at the tender age of sixteen and he did what was right in the eyes of the Lord and the Lord blessed him with victory after victory against his enemies and Uzziah grew strong. Because of this, his fame grew and spread across the lands. The problem was that once he was strong, his heart was lifted up in pride, and that caused his destruction.

In his pride, he had the audacity to enter the temple of the LORD to burn incense on the altar of incense. That was not his job. That was the job of the priests who had been consecrated to burn the incense on the altar of incense. When Uzziah was confronted by the priests telling him he was out of order, he became infuriated with the priests. And while he was angry with the priests, leprosy broke out on his forehead, and he was tossed out of the temple. He was unclean as a leper until the day he died and was cut off from the house of the LORD forever. As we just discussed, the forehead is the most prominent place on our bodies and God used Uzziah's leprous forehead as a billboard, advertising the seriousness of sin against the Lord and disrespecting His Holiness in serving out of order, advertising his allegiance was not to God, but to himself. Here we learn that 666 could also be said as self, self, self. So now we have learned that 666 could be said as man, flesh, self. Another way to express this would be me, me, me, or even as me, myself, and I.

The next thing the Lord showed me regarding foreheads and pride is completely awesome. It was the battle between David and the Philistine Goliath in 1Samuel 17. I'm sure we have all heard this story before numerous times. Goliath was a giant. He was a huge man of nine feet and was very strong. He took pride in the strength and ability of his flesh and boasted before God's people. Every day he called out to the Israelite army to send one man to fight him. He was so full of pride and of himself that he taunted them asking for just one man to fight him. He thought he was mighty enough to save men of both sides, by himself fighting just one man, and believing he was superior and not able to be defeated. Now, enter in David, a lowly shepherd boy who had a heart after God, who displayed God on His forehead, via dedicating his life to serving Him.

We all know how the story goes, but the Lord brought out things from this I hadn't thought of before. David defeated Goliath by picking up a stone. Jesus is our chief cornerstone. David hurled the stone at Goliath and hit him smack dab in middle of his forehead, and Goliath went down. He was done for. Goliath, in his pride, advertised himself, at the seat of his thoughts, or in other words, on his forehead, as being the greatest of men and that his gods were greater than the God of Israel having even cursed David by his gods. And it is through Jesus, our chief cornerstone that we battle and are delivered from the pride of self and from our flesh. This happens when we put Jesus on the seat or throne of our minds and body, on our foreheads. Thank you, Father! Thank you, Jesus!

Next, let's consider some other Scriptures pertaining to foreheads. Revelation 14:1 – Then I looked, and behold, a Lamb standing on Mount Zion, and with Him one hundred and forty-four thousand, having His Father's name written on their foreheads. And in Revelation 22:4 – They shall see His face, and His name shall be written on their foreheads. We also find the reference of the forehead in Revelation 7:2-3 – Then I saw another angel ascending from the east, having the seal of the living God. And he cried with a loud voice to the four angels to whom it was granted to harm the earth and the sea, saying, "Do not harm the earth, the sea, or the trees till we have sealed the servants of our God on their foreheads."

This Scripture confirms that God moves in sovereignty within seasons and waits until certain things are accomplished on the earth before He moves in a new thing or season. Here, the angels are to stay their hands until God's people, all that He pre-ordained before the foundation of the earth to be His, have received His seal, where? That's right, on their foreheads. It also speaks of the seal of God, so we would do well to understand what the seal of God is. John 6:27 – "Do not labor for the food which perishes, but for the food which endures to everlasting life, which the Son of Man will give you, because God the Father has set His seal on Him." Jesus has the seal of God, He is the firstborn among many brethren, so when we have Jesus living within us, we also have the seal of God, in also being children of God.

Now that this has been established, let's look at some more seal of God Scriptures. 2 Timothy 2:19 states, Nevertheless, the solid foundation of God stands, having this seal: "The Lord knows who His are," and "Let everyone who names the name of Christ depart from iniquity." 2 Corinthians 1:21-22 teaches – Now He who establishes us with you in Christ and has anointed us is God, who has also sealed us and given us the Spirit in our hearts as a guarantee. Also, Ephesians 4:30 says, And do not grieve the Holy Spirit of God, by whom you were sealed for the day of redemption. We also have Ephesians 1:13-14 – In Him you also trusted, after you heard the word of truth, the gospel of your salvation; in whom also, having believed, you were sealed with the Holy Spirit of promise, who is the guarantee of our inheritance until the redemption of the purchased possession, to the praise of His glory.

Let us now note three important elements we glean from these verses. They are inclusion, identity, and guarantee of inheritance. The first thing to understand is that because we are sealed, we have inclusion. We are included with Jesus. This means that because we belong to Him, then what He has belongs to us too. For example, because we are in Christ, His righteousness becomes our righteousness. We can find this in 2 Corinthians 5:21 – For He made Him who knew no sin to be sin for us, that we might become the righteousness of God in Him. We can also apply this same principle to His strength, His grace, His love, His compassion, His provision, and His power. Because we are included with Jesus, His ability works in us and through us because of the Holy Spirit that lives inside of us.

The second thing we learn is that we have our identity in Jesus. Because we are sealed, our identity is found in Christ. This means when God sees us, he identifies us as one of His very own, because we have been sealed. 1 Peter 2:9-10 says, But you are a chosen generation, a royal priesthood, a holy nation, His own special people, that you may proclaim the praises of Him who called you out of darkness into His marvelous light, who once were not a people but are now the people of God, who had not obtained mercy but now have obtained mercy. And Colossians 3:3 tells us, "for you died, and your life is hidden with Christ in God."

The third thing we are taught is that we are guaranteed an inheritance because we are the sealed of the Holy Spirit of God. Our eternity in heaven with Jesus is guaranteed, our salvation is guaranteed, and the forgiveness of all our sins is guaranteed. Although some of this isn't evident just yet, we can be confident it will happen because we have a seal or mark that God will honor. Thank you, Father God! Thank you, Jesus! Hallelujah!

This seal and mark of God is not just a New Testament concept. Even in the Old Testament, we find the mark of God on foreheads. Ezekiel 9:3-4 reads – Now the glory of the God of Israel had gone up from the cherub, where it had been, to the threshold of the temple. And He called to the man clothed in linen, who had the writer's inkhorn at his side; and the LORD said to him, "Go through the midst of the city, through the midst of Jerusalem, and put a mark on the foreheads of the men who sigh and cry out over all the abominations that are done within it." As you continue reading this account, you'll find those that had God's mark on their forehead, those who by deeds, advertised on their foreheads their allegiance was to God, were spared from His wrath.

This protection from the wrath of God for His people is something that He put into motion way back when He began to give commands to His people through Moses. When Moses was teaching the people of the significance of the festival of unleavened bread regarding their deliverance from Pharaoh and Egypt, and of teaching their children about it, he said in Exodus 13:8-9 – And you shall tell your son in that day saying, 'This is done because of what the LORD did for me when I came up from Egypt.' It shall be a as a sign to you on your hand and as a memorial between your eyes, (or forehead) that the LORD's law may be in your mouth; for with a strong hand the LORD has brought you out of Egypt." Now let's turn to Deuteronomy and have a look. Deuteronomy 6:5-8 reads – "You shall love the LORD your God with all of your heart, with all of your soul, and with all of your strength. And these words which I command you today shall be in your heart. You shall teach them diligently to your children and shall talk of them when you sit in your house, when you walk by the way, when you lie down, and when you rise up. You shall bind them as a sign on your hand, and they shall be as frontlets between your eyes. (Or in other words, on foreheads)

As a matter of fact, this concept and custom of the Jewish leaders is why the Pharisees wore phylacteries. Phylacteries were leather boxes containing Scripture passages and prayers and they were worn on the left arm, facing the heart, or on the forehead. This was a physical representation of the command of God given back in the Old Testament. However, those commands were figurative, to be a spiritual thing, a matter of the heart and mind. In Matthew 23:5, Jesus denounced the Pharisees wearing them, for they only wore them to be seen by men and demonstrate their zeal for "religion". Jesus said, "But all their works they do to be seen by men. They make their phylacteries broad…" They had completely missed the point that they were to memorize God's Word and keep it in their minds and hearts, thereby having His Word advertised on their foreheads, spiritually speaking, where God would see it and mankind would recognize it by their actions, lifestyle, and fruits. Jesus pointed out time after time that they were hypocrites, only serving themselves and thereby keeping the people from knowing the true heart of God.

Another thing you'll notice in the opening Scripture of this chapter is that the mark is either on the forehead or on the hand. Also, in the command of God through Moses in both the Exodus and Deuteronomy Scriptures, you'll notice the hand as well. This also is significant because as we previously learned, the cerebrum directly behind our foreheads is where we control all of our voluntary actions. It's where we instruct our hands in what to do. So let's take a look at some Scriptures pertaining to our hands for examples.

Psalms 9:16 – The LORD is known by the judgment He executes; the wicked is snared in the work of his own hands.

Psalm 24:3-4 – Who may ascend into the hill of the LORD? Or who may stand in His holy place? He who has clean hands and a pure heart.

Psalm 28:4 – Give them according to their deeds, and according to their wickedness of their endeavors; give them according to the work of their hands; render to them what they deserve.

Proverbs 6:16-19 – These six things the LORD hates, yes seven are an abomination to Him: A proud look, a lying tongue, hands that shed innocent blood, a heart that devises wicked plans, feet that are swift in running to evil, a false witness who speaks lies, and one who sows discord among the brethren.

Proverbs 12:14 – A man will be satisfied with good by the fruit of his mouth, and the recompense of a man's hands will be rendered to him.

Proverbs 31:19 – ... She extends her hand to the poor, yes she reaches out her hands to the needy.

Revelation 9:20-21 – But the rest of mankind, who were not killed by these plagues, did not repent *of the works of their hands*, that they should not worship demons and idols of gold, silver, brass, stone and wood, which can neither see nor hear nor walk. And they did not repent of their murders or their sorceries or their sexual immorality or their thefts.

　　In the above Scriptures, you'll notice hands doing both evil and good, or in other words, bearing bad fruit or good fruit. I give God praise and stand back in awe at the things He is revealing through the Holy Spirit in order for us to have understanding regarding His Word pertaining to 666. The things He is revealing is just blowing my mind at how awesome and all-encompassing He and His Word truly are! And as my pastor recently told me, "There is no better time to have your mind blown by God than now, in this present season." Hallelujah!

Now let's focus on the word "causes". The Scripture says, "He (the beast from the earth) causes all..." In the original Greek, the word causes is the word Poieo, and as a verb, like in this Scripture, means "to make to do" and is used of the bringing forth of fruit: Matthew 3:8 says, "Therefore, bear fruits worthy of repentance." For cross reference we can look at verse 10 of the same chapter where John the Baptist is speaking to the hypocritical Sadducees and Pharisees – "And even now the ax is laid to the root of the trees. Therefore every tree which does not bear good fruit is cut down and thrown into the fire." So we learn that the beast causes them to receive a mark on their hands and/or foreheads by bearing bad fruit. A good tree cannot bear bad fruit nor can a bad tree bear good fruit.

We also can see this in Matthew 7:15-20 where Jesus tells us we will know them by their fruits. It reads – "Beware of false prophets, who come to you in sheep's clothing, but inwardly are ravenous wolves. You will know them by their fruits. Do men gather grapes from thornbushes or figs from thistles? Even so every good tree bears good fruit, but a bad tree bears bad fruit. A good tree cannot bear bad fruit. Every tree that does not bear good fruit is cut down and thrown into the fire. Therefore by their fruits you will know them."

We learn in Galatians 5:19-23, what bad and good fruit are. It says – Now the works of the flesh (bad fruit) are evident, which are: adultery, fornication, uncleanness, lewdness, idolatry, sorcery, hatred, contentions, jealousies, outbursts of wrath, selfish ambitions, dissensions, heresies, envy, murders, drunkenness, revelries, and the like; of which I tell you beforehand, just as I also told you in time past, that those who practice such things will not inherit the kingdom of God. But the fruit of the Spirit is love, joy, peace, longsuffering, kindness, goodness, faithfulness, gentleness, self-control. Against such there is no law.

We'll discuss the above in more depth in an upcoming chapter but let's now take a look at some more Scripture about foreheads so that we may gain greater understanding of what the Spirit is teaching. Revelation 14:9-10 – Then a third angel followed them, saying with a loud voice, "If anyone worships the beast and his image, and receives his mark on his forehead or on his hand, he himself shall also drink of the wine of the wrath of God, which is poured out full strength into the cup of His indignation. He shall be tormented with fire and brimstone in the presence of the holy angels and in the presence of the Lamb. There is also Revelation 17:5 – And on her forehead a name was written: MYSTERY, BABYLON THE GREAT, THE MOTHER OF HARLOTS AND OF THE ABOMINATIONS OF THE EARTH.

To reiterate that this is not only something to come in the future, but has already been happening, let's turn to Jeremiah 3:1, and 3. "…But you have played the harlot with many lovers…you have a harlot's forehead; you refuse to be ashamed…" The word of the LORD had come to Jeremiah, and this is what the LORD said. It was in reference to Israel turning their hearts from following God to following the dictates of their evil hearts and joining themselves to the wicked ways of the world. They dethroned God from their hearts and minds and set *themselves* on their throne, and in so doing, by default, they allowed the devil to be seated on the throne of their hearts and minds. Therefore, they advertised a harlot's forehead. We also learn here that the heart is of utmost importance in our relationship with God, so we'll take a look at it in more depth in an upcoming chapter.

Now, let's look once again at the significance of the marks we display on our foreheads so that we can totally and completely understand what the Spirit is teaching here. Revelation 13:16-18 – He causes all, both small and great, rich and poor, free and slave, to receive a mark on their right hand or on their foreheads, and that no one may buy or sell except one who has the mark or the name of the beast, or the number of his name. Here is wisdom. Let him who has understanding calculate the number of the beast, for it is the number of a man: His number is 666. In comparison, Revelation 7:2-3 – Then I saw another angel ascending from the east, having the seal of the living God. And he cried with a loud voice to the four angels to whom it was granted to harm the earth and the sea, saying, "Do not harm the earth, the sea, or the trees till we have sealed the servants of our God on their foreheads."

We learn here that just as the seal of God and the divine name on believers foreheads signify God's own children and the Spiritual protection of them, so the mark of 666 signifies those who belong to the devil, the beast, via default of worshipping self. The 666 mark on the forehead is a symbolic way of describing utter loyalty, a mark of ownership and allegiance. It is a spiritual/ideological commitment, with a seal of fervent faithfulness to one's self in the exact same way that the seal of God on believers' foreheads shows their absolute loyalty and faithfulness to God the Father and Jesus.

CHAPTER SEVEN

BEWARE OF PHILOSOPHY

Colossians 2:6-10 – As you therefore have received Christ Jesus the Lord, so walk in Him, rooted and built up in Him and established in the faith, as you have been taught, abounding in it with thanksgiving. Beware lest anyone cheat you through philosophy and empty deceit, according to the tradition of men, according to the basic principles of the world, and not according to Christ. For in Him dwells all of the Godhead bodily; and you are complete in Him, who is the head of all principality and power.

Here, Paul is speaking to the Colossians and exhorting them to beware of others who would try to cheat them out of all that is theirs in Jesus by deceit and philosophies and traditions of men. As we have been discovering about 666 being as man-flesh-self, or me-myself-and I, through those eyes, let's look at a prevalent philosophy of men that is gaining much ground in the times we are living in. It is the philosophy of humanism which some have gone so far as to make a "religion."

Let's first look at the definition of philosophy from Webster's Dictionary. "The study of ideas about knowledge, truth, the meaning of life, etc. A particular set of ideas about knowledge, truth, the meaning of life, etc. A set of ideas about how to do something or how to live." Next, let's look at the definition of humanism. It's defined as a doctrine, attitude, or way of life, centered on human values; a philosophy that stresses an individual's dignity and worth and capacity for self-realization through reason. We should next look at the "philosophy of humanism" definition.

The definition from Webster's Dictionary describes the philosophy of humanism as, "a doctrine, an attitude, or way of life centered on human interests or values. Especially a philosophy that rejects supernaturalism (any form of any deity) and stresses an individual's dignity and worth and capacity for self-realization (fulfillment by oneself of the possibilities of one's character or personality) through reason. It is viewed especially as relying on reason, logic and naturalism (action, inclination, or thought and instincts; a theory denying that any event or object has a supernatural significance, that scientific laws are adequate to account for all phenomena) based on only natural desires as opposed to religious dogma."

Whew! After all of that, I think it is safe to say that humanists place importance on the pursuit of a self-defined meaningful and happy life and that they can do all things through their own power, talents, abilities and intelligence, or in other words, their own selves! Sounds like they have fallen victim to that very first temptation of you will be like God, or in other words, your own god. The main emphasis is on self and collectively, selves. But this is warned about in 1 Corinthians 3:18-23 – Let no one deceive **himself**. If anyone among you seems to be wise in this age, let him become a fool that he may become wise. For the wisdom of this world is foolishness with God. For it is written, "He catches the wise in their own craftiness.", and again, "The Lord knows the thoughts of the wise, that they are futile." Therefore, let no one boast in men. For all things are yours: whether Paul or Apollos or Cephas, or the world or life or death, or things present or things to come—all are yours. And you are Christ's, and Christ is God's.

And yet, out in society today, we keep hearing more and more words pertaining to self. We hear self-care, self-made, self-love, self-aware, self-hood, self-define, self-direction, self-identify, selfist, etc. This world of "self-everything" is a slippery slope. It is screaming from the rooftops that everybody should live for themselves and onto themselves. However, since every self-elevating person is able to self-choose what is right, many divisions and even wars have risen and continue to rise up and is taking society down, having been built on sinking sand and not on a solid foundation. In order to discover what solid foundation we should be building on regarding self, we need to turn to the Scriptures.

James 3:14-16 says – But if you have bitter envy and self-seeking in your hearts, do not boast and lie against the truth. This wisdom does not descend from above, but it is earthly, sensual, demonic. For where envy and self-seeking exist, confusion and every evil thing are there. Romans 2:8 says – but to those who are self-seeking and do not obey the truth but obey unrighteousness—indignation and wrath. Philippians 2:3 exhorts – Let nothing be done through selfish ambition or conceit, but in lowliness of mind, let each esteem others better than himself. What about Jesus? What did He say? Mark 12:30-31 answers that question – "And you shall love the LORD your God with all your heart, with all your soul, with all your mind, and with all your strength. This is the first commandment. And the second like it, is this: You shall love your neighbor as yourself. There is no other commandment greater than these." As you can clearly see, the lifting up of self is completely contrary to the Word of God.

As I was praying and seeking the Lord about what He wanted revealed about the philosophy of men, He reminded me that just as He is the Godhead consisting of the Father, the Son, and the Holy Spirit, we were created in His image and have three parts to us as well. I heard Him say, "In order to understand the number of man, and the philosophy of man, you need to fully understand the three separate parts of man." See, the terms soul and spirit have been discussed at length in philosophy and literature, and in the writings of various "religions". They're sometimes used interchangeably because people believe they're the same thing, but they are not.

So, let's turn to the Scriptures to discover them. 1 Thessalonians 5:23 says "Now may the God of peace Himself sanctify you completely; and may your whole spirit, soul, and body be preserved blameless at the coming of our Lord Jesus Christ." This tells us human beings are composed of three separate parts—spirit, soul, and body. The body is clearly different from the soul and in the same way, the soul is also different from the spirit. Hebrews 4:12 says "For the word of God is living and powerful, and sharper than any two-edged sword, piercing even to the division of soul and spirit, and of joints and marrow, and is a discerner of the thoughts and intents of the heart." The joints and marrow in our physical body are closely related in that they both are part of the bones that make up our skeletal system, but they're distinct and can be separated. In the same way, our soul and our spirit can be divided by the Word of God, showing that they're also distinct from each other.

The word soul in the original Greek is psuke, the same as our word psyche, which is the entire mind, both conscious and unconscious. The scientific study of the mind is known as psychology, and from it stems philosophy and has a long history of usage dating back to ancient Biblical times. Philosophers were very prevalent in the time when Paul went and shared the gospel with the Greeks. The problem with psychology and philosophy is that they try to lump together the soul and the spirit as one, while the Word distinctly shows us they are two separate things. The soul and the spirit are the two primary intangible or invisible parts of us that Scripture assigns to mankind. The word spirit refers to one of the invisible facets of man. All human beings have a spirit, but we are not spirits. However, in Scripture, only saved believers are said to be spiritually alive. Let's take a look at some of those verses. 1Corinthians 2:11-12 reads – For what man knows the things of man except the spirit of the man which is in him? Even so no one knows the things of God except the Spirit of God. Now we have received, not the spirit of the world, but the Spirit who is from God, that we might know the things that have been feely given to us by God.

The Scriptures also teach us that in contrast, unbelievers are spiritually dead. Ephesians 2:1, and 5 state – And you He made alive, who were dead in trespasses and sins…even when we were dead in trespasses, made us alive together with Christ (by grace you have been saved). Also, in Colossians 2:13 – And you, being dead in your trespasses and in the uncircumcision of your flesh, He has made alive together with Him, having forgiven you all trespasses. Paul also teaches us that the spiritual is essential to the life of believers. 1 Corinthians 2:14; 3:1 – But the natural man does not receive the things of the Spirit of God, for they are foolishness to him; nor can he know them, because they are spiritually discerned. And – And I, brethren, could not speak to you as to spiritual people but to carnal, as to babes in Christ. Ephesians 1:3; 5:19 say – Blessed be the God and Father of our Lord Jesus Christ, who has blessed us with every spiritual blessing in the heavenly places. And – speaking to one another in psalms and hymns and spiritual songs, singing and making melody in your heart to the Lord.

We also have Colossians 1:9 – "For this reason we also, since the day we heard it, do not cease to pray for you, and to ask that you may be filled with the knowledge of His will in all wisdom and spiritual understanding." The spirit is the facet in us that gives us the ability to have an intimate relationship with God. Whenever the word spirit is used, it refers to the invisible part of us that "connects" with God, who Himself is Spirit. John 4:23-24 – Jesus says, "But the hour is coming, and now is, when the true worshippers will worship the Father in spirit and truth; for the Father is seeking such to worship Him. God is Spirit, and those who worship Him must worship in spirit and truth." See, when we were born again, we were born of the Spirit in our human spirit, not in our soul. We received the Lord, and He came to live in our spirit.

Now that we've seen that the soul and spirit are different, we need to realize their functions also are different. The function of our spirit, the deepest part of our being, is related to the spiritual realm. It enables us to get in touch with, communicate with, and receive God Himself, as we just learned in John 4. God being Spirit means His substance is Spirit. Our spirit is the part of our being that corresponds to God and has the ability to get in touch with, fellowship with, and worship Him. Jesus teaches us this in John 3:5-6 – Jesus answered, "Most assuredly, I say to you, unless one is born of water and the Spirit, he cannot enter the kingdom of God. That which is born of the flesh is flesh, and that which is born of the Spirit is spirit."

We can see an example of communication of Spirit to spirit in Matthew 16:13-17 – When Jesus came into the region of Caesarea Philippi, He asked His disciples, saying, "Who do men say that I am? So, they said, "Some say John the Baptist, some Elijah, and others Jeremiah or one of the prophets." He said to them, "But who do you say that I am." Simon Peter answered and said, "You are the Christ, the Son of the living God." Jesus answered and said to him, "Blessed are you, Simon Bar-Jonah, for flesh and blood has not revealed this to you, but My Father who is in heaven." Here we find God's Spirit communicated with Peter's spirit.

So, what about our soul? Our soul is composed of our mind, will, and emotions. God's purpose in creating human beings with a spirit and a soul was so we would receive Him in our spirit and express Him through our soul. God created us with these faculties so that we can express Him to the world around us. We believers have the Spirit of God living in our spirit. So now, God wants us to live and act not all by ourselves, that is, by only our soul commanding our flesh body, but by His life in our spirit. So, as we go about throughout our day, we have to realize we can either live according to our natural human life in our soul and flesh, or by the life of Jesus in our spirit. We can easily live and act apart from the Lord in our soul, according to our own thoughts or feelings. When this happens, we express ourselves. But when we live by the Spirit of God in our spirit, Jesus is the source of our living, and the thoughts, feelings, and intentions of our soul are directed by our spirit. Then by our words and our actions, (by the fruit we bear), we express God.

Also, as we just touched on, our soul is made up of three parts—the mind, the will, and emotions. Proverbs 2:10-11 says, – When wisdom enters your heart, And knowledge is pleasant to your soul, Discretion will preserve you; Understanding will keep you."

Because knowledge is a matter of the mind, we see that the mind is a part of the soul. Proverbs 19:21 shows us this as well. It reads, – There are many plans in a man's heart, Nevertheless the LORD's counsel—that will stand. As well as Proverbs 24:14 – So shall the knowledge of wisdom be to your soul; If you have found it, there is a prospect, And hope will not be cut off. We see it in Psalms too. Psalm 139:14 – I will praise You, for I am fearfully and wonderfully made; Marvelous are Your works, And that my soul knows very well. Since to know is a matter of the mind, this also establishes that the mind is a part of the soul.

Psalm 13:2 speaks of taking counsel in the soul. – How long shall I take counsel in my soul, Having sorrow in my heart daily? How long will my enemy be exalted over me? Taking counsel is something considered in the mind. Also, Leviticus 26:15 says, "My soul still remembers And sinks within me." This indicates that the soul can remember things, therefore verifying the mind is indeed part of the soul.

The second part of the soul is the will. Job 7:15 says, "So that my soul chooses strangling And death rather than my body." And Job 6:7 says, "My soul refuses to touch them; They are loathsome food to me." To choose and to refuse are both choices of the will. Here we see that the will is also a part of the soul. Now let's look at 1 Chronicles 22:19 – "Now set your heart and your soul to seek the LORD your God…" Just as we set our mind to think, here we find we set our soul to seek. When we set our soul to do something, we are willing ourselves to do it. It's a matter of willpower, showing us again that the will is part of our soul.

The third part of the soul is the emotions. Our emotions encompass many feelings, including love, hatred, joy, and bitterness, just to mention just a few. These are just scratching the surface of all of the emotions we can feel in our soul, but we'll look at some verses involving the ones I have mentioned. Song of Solomon 3:4 KJV reads – It was but a little that I passed them, but I found him who my soul loveth…" And Psalm 42:1 – As the deer pants for the water brooks, So pants my soul for You, O God. These passages show us that to love is a function of the soul.

2 Samuel 5:8 reads – Now David said on that day, "Whoever climbs up by way of the water shaft and defeats the Jebusites (the lame and the blind, who are hated by David's soul) … Psalm 107:18 says, – Their soul abhorred all manner of food… and in Leviticus 26:15 God says – "and if you despise My statutes, or if your soul abhors My judgments…" In these Scriptures we find that the emotions of hating, despising and abhorring are also in the soul.

Isaiah 61:10 shows us that joy is of the soul. – "I will greatly rejoice in the LORD, My soul shall be joyful in My God…", as well as Psalm 35:9 – "And my soul shall be joyful in the LORD; It shall rejoice in His salvation. Then we have Job 3:20 – "Why is light given to him who is in misery, And life to the bitter of soul…" which shows us that bitterness is also of the soul.

With our soul, we think, reason, consider and remember and therefore we make decisions and choices. When we're born again, God's Holy Spirit regenerates our spirit by joining to it. He then continues on to our soul or mind, and transforms and renews it via His Word, and from there, our bodies are revitalized in Jesus, the very Word of God. We could also say that man consists of physical matter, a body that can be seen and touched. But he is also made up of intangible material that cannot be seen or touched, the spirit and soul. Our soul includes our intellect, will, emotions, conscious, and mind. These exist beyond our bodies' physical life on earth and are eternal. The spirit is our communication channel to God through the Holy Spirit. The word "spirit" can be defined as that part of a man related to worship and divine communion with God. It is through our spirit that we have "God-consciousness" and a relationship with Him. And it is the means through which spiritual gifts are given and manifested by the Holy Spirit.

1 Cor. 2:9-13 says – But as it is written: "Eye has not seen, nor ear heard, nor have entered the heart of man the things which God has prepared for those who love Him." But God has revealed them to us through His Spirit. For the Spirit searches all things, yes, the deep things of God. For what man knows the things of man except the spirit of the man which is in him? Even so no one knows the things of God except the Spirit of God. Now we have received, not the spirit of the world, but the Spirit who is from God, that we might know the things that have been freely given to us by God. These things we also speak, not in words which man's wisdom teaches but which the Holy Spirit teaches, comparing spiritual things with spiritual. Our spirit translates the things of the Spirit of God for our physical benefit.

In dissecting the three parts that make up man, the Lord showed me that in knowing this, we can double down on 666 being "man, man, man" in being specific in the three parts of man: 6, the spirit of man, 6, the soul of man, and 6, the body of man.

Now let's discuss the heart. Back in Biblical times, the people believed the heart is where we feel feelings and think thoughts. They thought it was the seat of intelligence and because they often used physical things to explain abstract concepts, they believed the heart was a metaphor for the mind, for all mental and emotional activity. So, when we read about the heart in the Bible, it is about the place where we have our will, our attitude and intentions, and that which is the source of our thoughts, actions and words.

Our hearts encompass our soul, our mind, will, and emotions as well as our spirits. It encompasses our character. It is the core of who we really are. It's our innermost being. In essence, our hearts are the real us. My heart is the totality of me and your heart is the totality of you. Let's take a look at some heart Scriptures that show us this. We have Deuteronomy 30:6 – "And the LORD your God will circumcise your heart and the heart of your descendants, to love the LORD your God with all of your heart and with all of your soul, that you may live." Jeremiah 15:16 – Your words were found and I ate them, and Your word was to me the joy and rejoicing of my heart. Jeremiah 17:9-10 – "The heart is deceitful above all things, and desperately wicked; Who can know it? I the LORD search the heart, I test the mind, even to give every man according to his ways, according to the fruit of his doing. Proverbs 14:33 – Wisdom rests in the heart of him who has understanding, but what is in the heart of fools is made known. Psalm 10:3-4 – For the wicked boasts of his heart's desire; He blesses the greedy and renounces the LORD. The wicked in his proud countenance does not seek God; God is in none of his thoughts. (Not on his forehead.) Proverbs 23:7 – For as he thinks in his heart, so is he...Psalm 51:10 – Create in me a clean heart, O God and renew a steadfast spirit within me. Psalm 66:18 – If I regard iniquity in my heart, The Lord will not hear. Ezekiel 36:26 – "I will give you a new heart and put a new spirit within you; I will take the heart of stone out of your flesh and give you a heart of flesh.

Next, let's take a look at some New Testament Scriptures pertaining to our heart. Matthew 13:19 – "when anyone hears the word of the kingdom, and does not understand it, the wicked one comes and snatches away what was sown in his heart... Romans 1:21 – Because, although they knew God, they did not glorify Him as God, nor were thankful, but became futile in their thoughts, and their foolish hearts were darkened. Romans 10:8-10 But what does it say? "The word is near you, in your mouth and in your heart" (that is, the word of faith which we preach): that if you confess with your mouth the Lord Jesus and believe in your heart that God has raised Him from the dead, you will be saved. For with the heart one believes unto righteousness, and with mouth confession is made unto salvation. Timothy 1:5 – Now the purpose of the commandment is love from a pure heart, from a good conscience, and from sincere faith.

Next, we'll look at Proverbs 4:23 – Keep your heart with all diligence, for out of it spring the issues of life. This Scripture sums it up perfectly. Throughout the Scriptures, the heart is often depicted as the seat of the thoughts, the will, the conscience and the emotions of mankind. The heart is the storehouse for wisdom and all that influences the life and the character of each and every one of us. And Jesus reminds us that we should love the Lord our God with all our heart, soul, mind and strength, with every part of our inner being. We have been endowed with reason and choices, with emotions and a will, which all abound in our hearts – and we have been given them by God to first glorify Him and secondly, to improve and develop our own lives.

With our heart we choose between good and evil. Our conscience sends out a message of whether something is right or wrong, and our heart is what drives us to choose. A heart that is in communication with God is able to choose the good every time. The heart that opens itself to other, impure influences becomes blind and confused when it comes to discerning between good and evil. From all of the above Scriptures, we can see that the heart is the totality of all we are. We therefore need to guard it with everything within us. When we do that, we can then guard ourselves against the philosophy of men. Thank you, Father for your Word and for bringing us understanding. May we all guard our hearts with all diligence.

CHAPTER EIGHT

SON OF PERDITION IS A DECISION

The term "son of perdition" is mentioned only twice throughout the Bible. The first time is in John 17:12 during Jesus' prayer to the Father regarding the disciples. It reads, "While I was with them in the world, I kept them in Your name. Those whom You have given Me, I have kept; and none of them is lost except the son of perdition, that the Scripture might be fulfilled." Here Jesus is referring to Judas Iscariot, who betrayed him.

Now let's take a look at Judas through the eyes of the Scriptures before he betrayed Jesus. Let's start in John 12, verses 3-6 – Then Mary took a pound of very costly oil of spikenard, anointed the feet of Jesus, and wiped his feet with her hair. And the house was filled with the fragrance of oil. But one of His disciples, Judas Iscariot, Simon's son, who would betray Him, said, "Why was this fragrant oil not sold for three hundred denarii and given to the poor?" This he said, not that he cared for the poor, but because he was a thief, and had the money box; and he used to take what was put in it. We also find that Matthew 26:14-16 says – Then one of the twelve, called Judas Iscariot, went to the chief priests and said, "What are you willing to give me if I deliver Him (Jesus) to you?" And they counted out to him thirty pieces of silver. So, from that time he sought opportunity to betray Him.

From these two verses, we learn that Judas was all about himself. He put himself first before the poor, and even before Jesus. Judas was one of the twelve disciples; he listened to every teaching of Jesus and saw every miracle Jesus performed. Luke 9:1-2 tells us that Jesus called the twelve disciples together, including Judas, and gave them power and authority over all demons and to heal others, to cure diseases, and yet, Judas chose himself instead, and betrayed Jesus.

Let's now look at Luke 22:3-4 – Then Satan entered Judas, surnamed Iscariot, who was numbered among the twelve. So, he went his way and conferred with the chief priests and captains how he might betray Him to them. And now let's look at John 13:26-27. Here, Jesus had just announced to the twelve that one of them would betray Him. Some of the disciples asked Him who it was and – Jesus answered, "It is he to whom I shall give a piece of bread when I have dipped it." And having dipped the bread, He gave it to Judas Iscariot, the son of Simon. Now after the piece of bread, Satan entered him. Then Jesus said to him, "What you do, do quickly."

When the Scriptures say that Satan entered Judas, doesn't it make you wonder how? Let's now see what Paul teaches in Ephesians 2:1-3 – And you He made alive, who were dead in trespasses and sins, in which you once walked according to the course of this world, according to the prince of the power of the air, the spirit that now works in the sons of disobedience, among whom also we all once conducted ourselves in the lusts of our flesh, fulfilling the desires of the flesh and of the mind, and were by nature children of wrath, just as the others. The key word we need to see here is the mind. See, Judas stole money because he loved money and the power and pleasures it could buy for him. As Paul shares in the above Scripture, Judas was dead in his sins, walking in the passions of his flesh, carrying out the desires of his body and mind and therefore following the prince of the power of the air. And when Satan saw his chances in Judas for his own awful schemes, he took them and entered Judas' mind.

So then, from the above Scriptures, we learn that because Judas chose himself, he gave the devil power over him through living in the lust of his flesh and mind. He therefore made himself sit upon the throne of his mind and in so doing, by default in dethroning Jesus from it, gave the throne to the devil, became a child of the devil, and did the devil's bidding. Jesus said in John 8:44 – "You are of your father the devil, and the desires of your father you want to do. He was a murderer from the beginning, and does not stand in truth, because there is no truth in him. When he speaks a lie, he speaks from his own resources, for he is a liar and the father of lies. And 1 John 7-8 states – Little children, let no one deceive you. He who practices righteousness is righteous, just as He is righteous. He who sins is of the devil, for the devil has sinned from the beginning. For this purpose, the Son of God was manifested, that He might destroy the works of the enemy. It's very similar to what James 1:12-16 teaches – Blessed is the man who endures temptation; for when he has been approved, he will receive the crown of life which the Lord has promised to those who love Him. Let no one say when he is tempted, "I am tempted by God"; for God cannot be tempted by evil, nor does He Himself tempt anyone. But each one is tempted when he is drawn away by his own desires and enticed. Then, when desire has conceived, it gives birth to sin; and sin, when it is full-grown, brings forth death. Do not be deceived, my beloved brethren.

Now, let's take a look at someone else who allowed Satan to enter their mind. It is King David and occurred with the numbering of his men, or in other words, taking a census. 1 Chronicles 21:1 – Now Satan stood up against Israel and moved David to number Israel. Now taking a census isn't a sin within itself as the Bible teaches us in Numbers 1:1-4 – Now the LORD spoke to Moses in the Wilderness of Sinai, in the tabernacle of meeting, on the first day of the second month, in the second year after they had come out of the land of Egypt, saying, "Take a census of all the congregation of the children of Israel, by their families, by their fathers' houses, according to the number of names, every male individually, from twenty years old and above—all who are able to go to war in Israel. You and Aaron shall number them by their armies. And with you, there shall be a man from every tribe, each one the head of his father's house. In this case, God instructed Moses to take a census to determine how many men were fit for war. God commanded the census and did so for His purposes.

In 1 Chronicles 21:1, we find that Satan moved David to number Israel. Satan entered his mind and tempted David to number the men and when Satan is involved, being the great tempter, we know there will be a temptation to sin. 2 Samuel 24:1 states it like this – Again, the anger of the LORD was aroused against Israel, and He moved David against them to say, "Go number Israel and Judah." Some say this is contradictory in that one verse says Satan moved David and the other says God moved David, but it isn't. Remember, Satan is just a vehicle God uses to bring about His good purposes, just like in Job when God asked Satan if he had considered His servant Job. And also remember that God set the boundaries of what Satan could and could not do. It is the same thing here. God's intent was to reveal David's pride in placing his trust in the number of mighty men he had for battle, rather than realizing the battle is God's and is won not in the strength, power and might of men, but by the Spirit of the Lord of Hosts. It is God who searches the heart and tests the mind. We learn this in Jeremiah 17:10 – "I, the LORD, search the heart, I test the mind, even to give every man according to his ways, according to the fruit of his doings. "So God used Satan to tempt David, and David allowed Satan to enter his mind and tempt him to sin, and ultimately perform the sin.

So, we have seen two examples of Satan entering the mind of men. But there is a big difference here. David, when he realized he had sinned, asked for forgiveness and God used the whole thing to teach and mature David for the purposes God yet had for him. And because he repented, he was never referred to as a "son of perdition". 1 Chronicles 21:8 shows us that David repented before God. – So, David said to God, "I have sinned greatly, because I have done this thing; but now, I pray take away the iniquity of your servant, for I have done very foolishly." But not Judas, Judas did indeed realize he had sinned too and did feel remorse, but he didn't repent to the Lord, rather he went and confessed to priests who didn't care about Judas, and he then went and killed himself. Matthew 27:3-5 – Then Judas, His betrayer, seeing that He had been condemned, was remorseful and brought back the thirty pieces of silver to the chief priests and elders, saying, "I have sinned by betraying innocent blood." And they said, "What is that to us? You see to it!" Then he threw down the pieces of silver in the temple and departed and went and hanged himself. And so Judas became a son of perdition by his actions. We have learned that the devil tempts us in our minds, and we will delve deeper into that in a moment, but for now, we'll look at the other Scripture pertaining to "son of perdition".

The second time "son of perdition" is mentioned is in 2 Thessalonians, chapter 2. The setting is Paul coming to calm the fears of the Thessalonians as some had told them that they had missed the Day of the Lord, what we refer to as Jesus' second coming. Verses 1-4 read – Now brethren, concerning the coming of our Lord Jesus Christ and our gathering together to Him, we ask you, not to be soon shaken in mind or troubled, either by spirit or by word or by letter, as if from us, as though the day of Christ had come. Let no one deceive you by any means; for that Day will not come unless the falling away comes first, and the man of sin is revealed, the son of perdition, who opposes and exalts himself above all called God or that sits as God in the temple of God, showing himself that he is God.

When the Lord had me turn to this Scripture to show me what He was revealing, revelation hit me so intensely as I read verses 3 and 4, that my heart palpitated, I got chills all up and down my body, and my palms became sweaty. The presence of the Lord was incredibly strong and undeniable. Let's break it down the way the Spirit revealed it to me: Verse 3 – Let no one deceive you by any means; *that Day will not come* unless the falling away comes first, and the man of sin is revealed, the son of perdition. [The man of sin and the son of perdition = number of man being 666 = me, myself and I, encompassing, man, flesh, self!] who opposes and exalts HIMSELF above all that is called God [God the Father, God the Son, and God the Holy Spirit] or that is worshipped, so that he sits as God in the "temple of God" [1 Corinthians 6:19 – Or do you not know that your body is the temple of the Holy Spirit who is in you, whom you have from God, and you are not your own?], showing HIMSELF that he is God. Wow! Those who put THEMSELVES on the throne of their mind which controls their whole body, the temple of God the Holy Spirit, setting themselves up as their own god, or as God, are a "son of perdition"! Also note in the above Scripture, that he shows "himself" that he is God. Not that he shows the whole world he is God as some have taught in error in regard to "the antichrist" which we'll discuss in further detail in a moment.

And when you think about it, it isn't really that surprising as this is the exact same thing that the serpent tempted Adam and Eve with in the garden, the very first temptation that led to the very first sin. Let's take a look at it. Genesis 3:1-5 – Now the serpent was more cunning than any beast of the field which the LORD God had made. And he said to the woman, "Has God indeed said, 'You shall not eat of every tree in the garden'?" And the woman said to the serpent, "We may eat the fruit of the trees of the garden; but of the tree which is in the midst of the garden, God has said, 'You shall not eat it, nor shall you touch it, lest you die.'" Then the serpent said to the woman, "You shall not surely die. For God knows that in the day you eat of it your eyes will be opened and you will be like God..."

And Boom! There you have it. Satan tempts by deceiving lies, distorting the Word of God, enticing people to be like God, or in other words, to be their own God, serving and worshipping only THEMSELVES. And when they fall into that temptation of serving and worshipping self, they choose to be a son of perdition. If you'll notice, it is a choice, we get to decide. God gives us choices as we discussed in the first chapter. We get to decide and choose whom we will serve, either God or ourselves. It's been that way since the beginning. Adam and Eve got to choose and even Joshua presented the people with that choice in Joshua 24:14 – "And if it seems evil to you to serve the LORD, choose for yourselves this day whom you will serve...But as for me and my house, we will serve the Lord."

Since we have been discussing "son of perdition", we would do well in knowing what the word perdition means. So, what is perdition, exactly? Perdition, in the original Greek, means destruction and state of the damned. So, a "son of perdition" has doomed himself to eternal destruction or to damnation. We can turn to the Scriptures and find examples of damnation in the King James Version of the Word. In the New King James Version, the word substituted for damnation is condemnation. I have chosen the King James Version to show you this, as it just seems to be a more potent message as well as uses the word damnation which perdition means in the original Greek.

Matthew 23:14 – Woe unto you, scribes and Pharisees, hypocrites! For ye devour widows' houses, and for a pretense make a long prayer: therefore, ye shall receive the greater damnation.

Matthew 23:33 – Ye serpents, ye generation of vipers, how can ye escape the damnation of hell?

Mark 3:29 – But he that shall blaspheme against the Holy Ghost hath never forgiveness, but is in danger of eternal damnation:

John 5:28-29 – Marvel not at this; for the hour is coming, in the which all that are in the graves shall hear His voice. And shall come forth; they that have done good, unto the resurrection of life; and they that have done evil, unto the resurrection of damnation.

Romans 13:2 – Whosoever therefore resisteth the power, resisteth the ordinance of God: and they that resist shall receive to themselves damnation.

1 Corinthians 11:28-29 – But let a man examine himself, and so let him eat of that bread, and drink of that cup. For he that eateth and drinketh unworthily, eateth and drinketh damnation to himself, not discerning the Lord's body.

1 Timothy 5:12 – Having damnation, because they have cast off their first faith.

2 Peter 2:3 – And through covetousness shall they with feigned words make merchandise of you: whose judgment now of a long time lingereth not, and their damnation slumbereth not.

In reading these Scriptures, we can see how serious an issue it is to reject God and His plan of salvation through His Son Jesus and decide to live for self. Because when one does this, they become a son of perdition and doom themselves to eternal damnation. I know this ignites a fire within me to pray for the lost like never before, and I pray that it does for you as well. Amen!

Now let's take a look at how our minds are the gate that needs to be under watch and be protected at all times, to keep the enemy out. Every kingdom has gates that are either opened to receive or closed to keep out. Luke 17:21 reads, "…For indeed, the kingdom of God is within you." When we pray and seek the Kingdom of God, we are also praying for the rule and reign of the kingdom of God in our lives. This only happens when Jesus is in charge, when He sits upon the throne of our minds. When Jesus spoke this to the Pharisees in the above Scripture, who asked about the kingdom of God, Jesus was speaking of Himself. When we are under His Lordship, and when He is ruling in our life, that is the kingdom of God. Another thing to note is that when Jesus, in the flesh, was crucified, the Scripture tells us He was crucified at Golgotha, the place of a skull. This is important because the skull is what harbors our minds, and where we must crucify our flesh as well.

The battle that takes place in our minds is real. This is why Paul tells us in Ephesians 6 to put on the whole armor of God so that we can withstand the wiles or tricks of the enemy. We need to have the helmet of salvation on to guard our minds and keep its gate closed to the temptations of the devil. Salvation is when we repent of our sins and ask the Lord Jesus to be the Lord of our lives and sit upon the throne of our mind and heart. In keeping on our helmet of salvation for protection, we withstand the onslaught of worldly and evil thoughts and don't let them enter through our gate into our mind. How do we do that? We have to know the Word of God in order to do that. This is why Paul instructed us in Romans 12:2 to be transformed by the renewing of our minds. – And do not be conformed to this world, but be transformed by the renewing of your mind, that you may prove what is that good and acceptable and perfect will of God. And in Ephesians 4:23 – and be renewed in the spirit of your mind.

How do we continue to be renewed in our mind? By searching the Scriptures to see if what we have heard is in line with the Word of God. Let's take a look at Acts 17:11 – These (the people of Berea) were more fair-minded than those in Thessalonica, in that they searched the scriptures daily to find out whether these things we so. We also renew our minds by reading our Bibles on a regular basis, memorizing Scripture for reference, while we walk out our lives. See, once we have our minds renewed with the Word of God, we are then able to do battle in our minds as Paul instructs in 2 Corinthians 10:3-5 …we do not war according to the flesh. For the weapons of our warfare are not carnal but mighty in God for pulling down strongholds, casting down arguments and every high thing that exalts itself against the knowledge of God, bringing every thought into captivity to the obedience of Christ. When we know the Word of God, we can therefore stop those thoughts and arguments at the gate to our mind and banish them from trying to reside there. We take them captive and toss them out.

In speaking of the battling of thoughts in our mind and casting down arguments, I remembered such an incident when I was young. I know this is a simple thing and illustration, but it really does bring it home. I had been running errands with my dad and while we were out, he bought me a red "super" super ball. What I mean by that is this super ball was bigger than any I had ever seen before, about the same size as a baseball. So, there I was sitting on the couch in the living room with my super ball in hand, admiring it. I really wanted to see it "super" bounce, but because we lived on a dirt road and had a dirt driveway, I didn't have a hard surface "floor" outside to see it do its stuff without getting all dirty. I then noticed the big screen of the TV we had. It was one of those console TVs that were popular back in the 1970s. A thought entered my mind that I could throw my ball at the hard TV screen. Then another thought entered in telling me I could possibly break the screen and then I'd be in big trouble. Then another arguing thought, telling me I could just throw it lightly. But then I thought I wouldn't get the full "super" effect if I did that, so to just throw it hard. Another thought popped in telling me it wasn't worth the risk of breaking the TV screen. Then another thought was telling me, but I knew that I really, really, really wanted to do it, though. Back and forth these thoughts went like a ping pong match!

These dueling thoughts battled in my mind for a while. The struggle was real for a little nine-year-old girl! I am happy to tell you that I did not throw my ball at the TV screen. But that is how we battle temptation in our minds. If I had stopped the thought processes after the first temptation and countering thought and got myself up off the couch to go searching for something outside with a hard surface, I would have been done with it. But, because I even considered that opposing thought, imagining in my mind how cool it would be to see the ball bounce off the TV screen, wondering if I would be able to catch it after, or if it would hit the wall behind me, bounce to another wall, etc., I was giving those tempting thoughts a foothold. I had entered the danger zone. And the further down the danger zone we go, the more difficult it is to find our way back out. If I hadn't been interrupted by my dad calling for me to come outside though, who knows if I would have thrown my ball at the TV? We should be very thankful that we also have "a voice of the Father" to listen to as He calls to us as well, making a way of escape.

James 4:7 tells us – Therefore, submit to God. Resist the devil and he will flee from you. When we cast out high thoughts that exalt themselves over the knowledge of God, we are resisting the devil and he does have to flee. I know this to be true, as I have had to do this too many times to count. I can encourage you though, the more you do it, the easier it becomes. When we truly and fully grasp that we have power over all the works of the enemy as Jesus tells us we do, it just becomes second nature. Sometimes I relate it to a scene in *The Wizard of Oz* movie. It's when Glinda the good witch speaks to the wicked witch of the east. "You have no power here. Begone!" It is really just that simple. Paul tells us in 1 Corinthians 2, that the natural mind of man cannot receive the deep things of God because they are foolishness to him since they are spiritually discerned. We can receive those deep things however, when our minds have been renewed by the Spirit, because we then have the mind of Christ. When Jesus sits on the throne in our minds, the control center of our entire body, we have the mind of Christ, but if we put self on the throne, then by default, we are anti-Christ.

Speaking of antichrist, do you know what word you will not find in the entire Book of Revelation, from the first word through the last? The word "antichrist", it's not in there. And seeing as it is John who wrote the Book of Revelation as well as all of the Scriptures that refer to antichrist, you would think he would mention it in there, right? There is a reason he didn't, and it is because there is no "Antichrist" in the Book of Revelation. Let's turn to the Scriptures where John does mention the word antichrist to learn about it.

1 John 2:18, 22 – Little children, it is the last hour; and as you have heard that the Antichrist is coming, even now many antichrists have come, by which we know that it is the last hour. Verse 22 says – Who is a liar but he who denies that Jesus is the Christ? He is antichrist who denies the Father and the Son. Now let's look at 1 John 4:2-3 where John mentions antichrist again. It reads – By this you know the Spirit of God: Every spirit that confesses that Jesus Christ has come in the flesh is of God, and every spirit that

does not confess that Jesus has come in the flesh is not of God. And this is the "spirit of the Antichrist", which you have heard was coming, and is now in the world. Here we learn that there is a spirit of the Antichrist, or in other words, that the Antichrist is a spirit. Remember, Paul taught us that we fight not against flesh and blood, but against principalities, against powers, against the rulers of the darkness of this age, against spiritual hosts of wickedness in the heavenly places.

We also see that John was teaching there were many antichrists, and that antichrist is whoever denies Jesus Christ and Father God and that whoever denies them, is a liar. Those antichrists were obviously deceived by the spirit of antichrist. John also says that the people had heard that antichrist was coming. How can that be when John is the only one who mentions antichrist? Jesus Himself warned about false christs and false prophets arising before His second coming in Matthew 24:24. And in Matthew 7:15, He said to beware of false prophets who come to you in sheep's clothing, and that you would know them by their fruits. John again mentions antichrist in 2 John verse 7 – For many deceivers have gone out into the world who do not confess Jesus Christ as coming in the flesh. This is a deceiver and an antichrist. So, we learn that those who deny Jesus in either words or deeds (by their fruits) are an antichrist and the antichrist is a spirit, obviously not the Holy Spirit. Antichrist is not a specific person, but a spirit of the age consisting of ruling spirits, powers, and principalities.

Let's now look at 1 Timothy 4:1-2 – Now the Spirit expressly says that in the latter times, some will depart from the faith, giving heed to deceiving spirits and "doctrines of demons", speaking lies in hypocrisy, having their own conscious seared with a hot iron. Hmmm. Whoever received "revelation" about there being a specific person, "the antichrist" that is in charge of defeating and inflicting God's people throughout the Book of Revelation, and introduced and taught it to the church, must have received a doctrine of demons.

All throughout God's Word, He has shown time and time again that we, His people, are victorious in Him, that He is the Lord of hosts, and commands His hosts. Battle after battle His people are victorious in Him. Let's look at 2 Kings 6:15-17 – And when the servant of the man of God arose early and went out, there was an army, surrounding the city with horses and chariots. And his servant said to him, "Alas, my master! What shall we do?" So, he answered, "Do not fear, for those who are with us are more than those who are with them." And Elisha prayed, and said, "LORD, I pray, open his eyes that he may see." Then the LORD opened the eyes of the young man, and he saw. And behold, the mountain was full of horses and chariots of fire all around Elisha.

And we have Gideon in Judges 6. The Midianites had been coming and stealing all of the people's crops and livestock and the people were impoverished. Then the angel of the LORD comes to Gideon who was fearful of them and hiding wheat in the winepress. He addresses Gideon as a mighty man of valor and tells him to conquer the Midianites and that surely the LORD would be with him and he would defeat them. Here we find someone hiding in fear, and the LORD came, told him to be courageous, and his enemy would be defeated. And the enemy was defeated. God has not given us a spirit of fear, but of power and of love and a sound mind. 2 Timothy 1:7.

God has also shown that Jesus through his crucifixion, death, and resurrection, disarmed principalities and powers and made a spectacle of them, triumphing over them and has given that same power to us. Jesus proclaimed that He would build His church and the gates of Hell would not prevail against it. So then, why on earth, would Jesus reveal to John, in the Book of Revelation, for us, that we would be powerless against a spirit, the spirit of the antichrist, hiding out in fear right before His second coming where He would come to rescue us in the nick of time, like a comic book superhero? He wouldn't. He wouldn't want us to believe that at all because it is contrary to the rest of His Word. But who would? The devil would, wouldn't he? This most certainly falls under "doctrine of demons".

So the spirit of "son of perdition" and antichrist have entered minds that have allowed Satan in and think as Satan leads. Therefore, 666 could also be called an "antichrist seal".

Let's now re-cap. We have learned throughout this chapter, through the Word of God, that we choose whether we are going to be a son of perdition, advertising being ruled by self, flesh, me; advertising 666 on our foreheads, as opposed to choosing to be ruled by Jesus and having the mind of Christ and seal of God, full of power and authority. We choose if our minds either are for Christ or are antichrist. We choose to be a son of perdition and a lawless one or a child of the most high God, God the Father, God the Son, and God the Holy Spirit. It is our choice, our decision.

Thank you, Father, for shining your light of revelation into the darkness of deceit, and revealing Your Truth as You teach it throughout Your Word. Amen!

CHAPTER NINE

OVERCOMERS

As I was praying and seeking God as to what He wanted revealed to us next, He gave me the word "overcomers" which sent me on yet another journey through His Word to discover what He was speaking. So, the first thing I did was look up the word "overcome" in the original Greek. It is the word nikaw which means "to conquer, prevail, triumph, and overcome". It is found 28 times in 24 verses throughout the New Testament. We know that in order to conquer and prevail, we have to be involved in a battle. We've learned throughout the pages of this book, according to the Word of God, that we need to battle the deception and temptations of the enemy, to battle against the ways of the world, and to battle our own flesh, or in other words, our natural self. Therefore, we will be looking at the Scriptures that pertain to them.

Also, as we learned that the entire Word of God is all about Jesus, from beginning to end, we'll start in the Book of Genesis, and conclude in the Book of Revelation. In Genesis, we found the first temptation of the devil and it was a tempting to be like God, or to be as wise as God, therefore being able to be one's own ruler or god. Now let's look and see what God said to the devil, that deceiving serpent, because of this. It is the very first prophecy in the Word and the first promise of Jesus, for us. Genesis 3:14-15 – So the LORD God said to the serpent: "Because you have done this, You are cursed more than all cattle, And more than every beast of the field; On your belly you shall go, And you shall eat dust All the days of your life. And I will put enmity Between you and the woman, And between your seed and Her Seed; He shall bruise your head, And you shall bruise His heel. After reading the above Scripture, Roman's 16:20 popped into my head. – And the God of peace shall crush Satan under your feet shortly...

After the Lord gave me these Scriptures, He brought back a memory to me of when I was a child of ten years old. I hadn't thought of it since the time it happened because it just wasn't a big deal to me. But after He brought the incident back to my remembrance, He began to give me revelation concerning it. God is so awesome!

As I stated, I was ten years old, and it was summertime. We lived on a lake and my dad had just recently taught me to water-ski. To say I loved it would be an understatement as it was the most fun thing I had ever learned to do. Anyway, I was at my best friend's house visiting when their phone rang. After hanging up the phone, my best friend's mom told me that my dad had called to tell me that he wanted me to come home because it was time to go water-skiing.

At that, I was off. I took off running full speed down the side of our dirt road barefooted. It was a difficult thing for my parents to keep me in shoes during the summer. Every chance to be barefooted, I took, and this day was no different. I was only about four houses away from our house when I stepped on something sort of hard, but yet, sort of squishy. I felt whatever it was give way under my heel. I stopped running and turned around to see what I had stepped on knowing it wasn't a rock or an acorn because it was much too soft for that.

When I turned around and looked behind me, I found a little baby snake about six to eight inches long lying in the sand on the side of the road. I gently pushed it with my big toe but it didn't try to slither away or even move at all. I bent low and picked it up finding it was dead yet still pliable and somewhat warm to the touch, and that's when I knew for sure that it was what I had stepped on. I just had to show my dad, so I picked it up and continued toward home. When I arrived and showed it to my parents, they freaked out telling me it was a baby rattlesnake, pointing out the little rounded balls at the end of its tail. They told me I was lucky I crushed its head when I stepped on it because had my foot stepped further back or even next

to it, it could have bitten me and injected me with its deadly venom.
I just shrugged my shoulders while saying, "Oh, whoops!" Then I
proceeded into the house to change into my swimsuit so I could
water-ski.

After the Lord brought this back to my memory, I
immediately recognized the incident as Satan that serpent of old,
being crushed under our feet. I said, "Lord, that is so cool! You gave
me a mental object lesson."

The Holy Spirit answered, "But that isn't all of it. Let's look
deeper. First, you received a call from your father and heeded it.
Then, you responded in obedience and headed home to be about
your father's business which in this case was water-skiing. And as
you were about your father's business, your ordered step crushed the
head of the snake under the heel of your foot. You did not step
where you could have been hurt because it is I who guides your
steps".

And that is exactly how simple it is. When anyone heeds and
answers the call of the Father who chose them and walks with Him
in obedience with guided steps, being about the business of their
Father, serving in the Kingdom of God, on their journey 'home',
they crush the enemy under their feet. When the devil has no hold on
them, his attempts to entice and deceive them to sin are crushed.
Psalms 37:23 says, "The steps of a good man are ordered by the
LORD, and He delights in his way. And Proverbs 16:9 says, "A
man's heart plans his way, but the Lord directs his steps. Next, we'll
look at what Jesus said about it. Luke 10:19 – And He (Jesus) said to
them, "Behold, I give you the authority to trample on serpents and
scorpions, and over all the power of the enemy, and nothing shall by
any means hurt you." How much authority over the power of the
enemy did Jesus give us? He said all!

God is so amazing! I never would have put all of that
together from an insignificant experience I had when I was just a kid

and could never have dreamed that God would use it as an example of how things work in His Kingdom at hand. It also proves He is always with us, by our side, and that He indeed knows everything we will encounter in life from way back before he laid the foundation of the world. He orchestrated this event in my life knowing that it would be an example 49 years later as He led me to write this book! Hallelujah! Praise His mighty name!

Okay, to continue on discovering what the Word tells us about overcoming, prevailing, conquering, and triumphing in and through Jesus, let's look at John 16:33 where Jesus says – "These things I have spoken to you, that in Me you may have peace. In the world you will have tribulation; but be of good cheer, I have overcome the world." And at Romans 8:35-37 – Who shall separate us from the love of Christ? Shall tribulation, or distress, or persecution or famine, or sword? As it is written: "For your sake we are killed all day long; We are accounted as sheep for the slaughter." Yet in all these things we are more than conquerors through Him who loved us. What I want to point out in these Scripture verses other than being overcomers, is the word tribulation. Jesus told us we would have tribulation and that tribulation could not separate us from Him. Yet another reason we should not fear tribulation.

Next let's look at 2 Corinthians 2:14 – Now thanks be to God who always leads us in triumph in Christ, and through us diffuses the fragrance of His knowledge in every place. Next, Colossians 2:15 – Having disarmed principalities and powers, He made a public spectacle of them, triumphing over them in it. And now let's look at some Scripture from the Book of Revelation regarding overcoming. In Revelation 3:21, Jesus tells us – "To him that overcomes I will grant to sit with Me on My throne, as I also overcame and sat down with My Father on His throne." Revelation 5:5 – But one of the elders said to me, "Do not weep. Behold, the Lion of the tribe of Judah, the Root of David, has prevailed to open the scroll and to loose its seven seals. Revelation 17:14 – "These will make war with the Lamb, and the Lamb will overcome them, for He is Lord of lords and King of kings; and those who are with Him are called, chosen, and faithful." In these Scriptures, we find that Jesus is the Overcomer. Jesus is the source of our victory and the means through which we overcome. This is shown to us all throughout the Scriptures. It's all about Jesus as we previously learned, and now we can add to that it's all about Jesus being the Overcomer and teaching and leading us to be overcomers as well. Thank you, Jesus!

Now let's look at some Scriptures that show us how we become overcomers in Jesus. 1 John 4:4 says – You are of God, little children and have overcome them, because He (Jesus) who is in You is greater than he who is in the world. 1 John 5:4 says – For whatever is born of God overcomes the world. And this is the victory that has overcome the world—our faith. We'll dig into faith further in a moment, but first, let's refresh our minds about the other ways we've already discussed.

The first of those ways is by diligence and discipline over our flesh. Galatians 5:16 tells us – I say then: Walk in the Spirit, and you will not fulfill the lust of the flesh. Ephesians 5:18 tells us – And do not be drunk with wine, in which is dissipation; but be filled with the Spirit. Philippians 3:3 – For we are the circumcision, who worship God in Spirit, rejoice in Christ Jesus, and have no confidence in the flesh. Romans 13:14 tells us – But put on the Lord Jesus Christ and make no provision through the flesh. 1 Timothy 4:7 tells us – But reject profane and old wives' fables and exercise yourself toward godliness. And lastly, 2 Peter 1:3-8 – As His divine power has given to us all things that pertain to life and godliness, through the knowledge of Him who called us by glory and virtue, by which have been given to us exceedingly great and precious promises, that through these you may be partakers of the divine nature, having escaped the corruption that is in the world through lust. But also, for this very reason, giving all diligence, add to your faith virtue, to virtue knowledge, to knowledge self-control, to self-control perseverance, to perseverance godliness, to godliness brotherly kindness, and to brotherly kindness love.

Now let's get back to faith. Faith is of utmost importance, so much so, that God included an entire chapter about it in His Word. It's referred to as the faith hall of fame and is Hebrews chapter 11. Through faith, we accomplish amazing things. Faith is the opposite of fear, and the powers that be in our world today know this and are trying to overcome us by broadcasting fear mongering in every way possible. You need just turn on any news broadcast to see it. Also in their plan, they have included social media outlets and big tech and are even trying to paralyze you in fear through commercials. But we are not ignorant of their devices if we have our minds renewed and transformed by God's Word. Thank you, Lord!

As we have discovered, a false interpretation of the Book of Revelation is a doctrine of demons and was for the purpose of inflicting fear upon the saints. And it has unfortunately been taught in the church for absolutely years. But as we have entered into a season where God is shining His Light of Truth upon the doctrine of demons, worldly philosophies, and the traditions of men, so that we, His people, can arise and shine in the darkness of the world, let's take a look at some of those Scriptures that have been taught in error. Revelation 13:7 says – "It was granted to him to make war with the saints and overcome them. And authority was given over every tribe, tongue and nation." As I read that Scripture during my time of seeking the Lord, I heard Him say, "So what? This isn't anything new, as it has been happening all throughout My Word."

It was then I was reminded that the devil is only a pawn in God's plans and purposes, a tool, a vehicle in which He brings His purposes to pass. God granted power to the devil to make war with Job for His purposes. God granted power to Satan to make war with David for His purposes, God granted power to Satan to make war with Peter for His purposes and to make war with Judas for His purposes as well. This war is spiritual warfare. Paul teaches us in Ephesians 6:11-13 to – Put on the whole armor of God, that you may be able to stand against the wiles of the devil. For we do not wrestle with flesh and blood, but against principalities, against powers, against the rulers of darkness of this age, and spiritual wickedness in heavenly places. Therefore take up the whole armor of God, that you may be able to withstand in the evil day, and having done all, to stand.

We have found that Job overcame, David overcame, Peter overcame, but Judas did not. With Judas, Satan overcame. We learned back in chapter one of this book that God has given us choices. We get to choose what we seek and desire and whom we will serve. All of the men above chose God with the exception of Judas who chose the way of Satan. He chose to become a son of perdition, kicking Jesus off the throne of his mind and heart to thereby advertise 666 or self-flesh-me on his forehead and received his just reward for it, which was eternal damnation. And I am as sure as I can be, that power was granted to the enemy to make war with you as well, as was with me. But through faith, we choose Jesus and overcome! However, we if don't, and choose self, then we have granted the enemy power to overcome us. Again, we choose!

Now let's look at another verse that was misinterpreted to inflict fear within our hearts. It is Revelation 13:11-13 – He performs great signs, so that he even makes fire come down from heaven on the earth in the sight of men. And he deceives those who dwell on the earth by those signs which he was granted to do in the sight of the beast… And chapter 16:14 – For they are spirits of demons, performing signs, which go out to the kings of the earth and of the whole world…As I read these verses, the Lord said again, "So what? This also has happened before." I was reminded of when Moses and Aaron went before the Pharaoh and performed signs and wonders and up to a point, the Pharaoh's magicians performed the same ones as well. The awesome part is that God's power was way mightier than the magicians' power in sorcery and they could no longer replicate the signs and wonders God wrought, and therefore, God's glory was revealed. Hallelujah!

We can see another example in the New Testament in Acts 8:1-25. It's the story of a man named Simon who practiced sorcery and made his living by doing so. Then he encountered Philip and the apostles who were baptizing in the Holy Spirit and performing miracles and signs. So Simon believed and was water baptized himself. But when he saw that through the laying on of hands, the Holy Spirit was given and was the means for the performing of signs and miracles, he offered to pay money for it. He recognized the power of The Holy Spirit was more powerful than his sorcery. But Peter called him out for thinking that the gift of God could be bought and told him to repent because he was poisoned by bitterness and bound by iniquity and perhaps the thought of his heart may be forgiven him. See, Simon wanted to be able to be baptized in the Holy Spirit, performing signs and miracles not to make it all about Jesus, but rather to use it as a means for financial gain for himself. He chose to allow SELF to rule and reign over him as opposed to Jesus.

So, we know that demons can perform signs and miracles and that sorcery is in no way more powerful than God's power. We actually are warned about sorcery in many Scriptures throughout the Old and New Testaments. One instance in the Old, we find Moses' warning in Deuteronomy 13:1-3 – "If there arises among you a prophet or a dreamer of dreams, and he gives you a sign or a wonder, and the sign or the wonder comes to pass, of which he spoke to you, saying, 'Let us go after other gods'—which you have not known— 'and let us serve them,' "you shall not listen to the words of that prophet or that dreamer of dreams, for the LORD your God is testing you to know whether you love the LORD your God with all your heart and with all your soul." We also know that God allows these signs to be done by the enemy to test us just as He tested Job. We also see again where the devil is just a vehicle that God utilizes for His good purposes.

Now let's go back to the New Testament, to 2 Thessalonians 2:3-4 where Paul was assuring the Thessalonians they had not missed the second coming of the Lord Jesus Christ – Let no one deceive you by any means; for that day will not come unless the falling away comes first, and the man of sin is revealed, the son of perdition, who opposes and exalts himself above all that is called God, or that is worshipped, so that he sits as God in the temple of God, showing himself that he is God. We learned here that we choose to be a son of perdition by allowing our SELF to be the ruler of us, the temple of the Holy Spirit, rather than making Jesus that ruler.

Let's now continue on in verses 5-12 – Do you not remember that when I was still with you, I told you these things? And now you know what is restraining, that he may be revealed in his own time. For the mystery of lawlessness is already at work; only He who now restrains will do so until He is taken out of the way. And then the lawless one will be revealed, whom the Lord will consume with the breath of His mouth and destroy with the brightness of His coming. The coming of the lawless one is according to the working of Satan, with all power, signs, and lying wonders, and with all unrighteous deception among those who perish, because they did not receive the love of truth that they might be saved. And for this reason, God will send them strong delusion, that they should believe the lie, and they all may be condemned who did not believe the truth but had pleasure in unrighteousness.

Let's break this down with what we have learned. Paul said the mystery of lawlessness is already at work. This means that it was working then and is still working now, letting us know this is not a thing only of the future. Next, he says that He who is restraining will continue to until He is taken out of the way and then the lawless one, the man of sin, the son of perdition, will be revealed. Remember Revelation 7:2-3 says – Then I saw another angel ascending from the east having the seal of the living God. And He cried with a loud voice to the four angels to whom it was granted to harm the earth and the sea, saying, "Do not harm the earth, the sea, or the trees until we have sealed the servants of God on their foreheads." We know we receive the seal of God once we believe and ask Jesus to be the Lord of our lives. So, destruction cannot come until the very last person who was written in the Book of Life before the foundation of the world has come into Jesus' fold. This is a restraining. Jesus told his disciples that the gospel would be preached in all the world, then the end would come.

Now let's jump over to Revelation 9:4 – They were commanded not to harm the grass of the earth, or any green thing, or any tree, but only those men who do not have the seal of God on their forehead. It is at this point that the lawless one, the son of perdition is revealed. All that are left who do not have the seal of God on their foreheads, but have chosen, rather, to live for self, satisfying their flesh, advertising me-myself-I, or 666 on their foreheads, are remaining and thus revealed. These are the ones that will be consumed by the breath of the Lord's mouth and destroyed with the brightness of His coming.

Let's revisit Revelation 19 and read verses 11-16 – Now I saw heaven opened, and behold, a white horse. And He who sat on him was called Faithful and True, and in righteousness He judges and makes war. His eyes were like a flame of fire, and on His head were many crowns. He had a name written that no one knows except Himself. He was clothed with a white robe dipped in blood, and His name is called The Word of God. And the armies in heaven, clothed in white linen, white and clean, followed Him on white horses. Now out of His mouth goes a sharp sword, that with it He should strike the nations. And He Himself will rule them with a rod of iron. He Himself treads the winepress of the fierceness and wrath of Almighty God. And He has on His robe and on His thigh a name written: KING OF KINGS AND LORD OF LORDS. We know Him to be Jesus.

As we have learned, God's Word is Jesus and is all about Jesus and we should make our lives all about Jesus. It is really that simple. We are either all about Jesus or all about ourselves. We either have the mind of Christ or we are antichrist. We either have advertised on our foreheads or minds, the seal of God, or man-self-flesh, me-me-me, the mark of the beast, 666. It really isn't complicated. Romans 14:7 – For none of us lives to himself, and no one dies to himself. For if we live, we live to the Lord; and if we die, we die to the Lord. Therefore, whether we live or die, we are the Lord's. For to this end Christ died and rose and lived again, that He might be Lord of both the dead and the living. Jesus Himself said it was that simple in Matthew 16:25. I'm going to present this in the Amplified version as I like how it makes it plain. – For whoever wishes to save his life [in this world] will [eventually] lose it [through death], but whoever loses his life [in this world] for My sake will find it [that is, life with Me for all eternity]. Hallelujah! Thank you, Father!

When we live for Jesus, we do not live for self. We should be watchful because self is the sure path to all the evils of a fallen and lost state and world. When we are operating in the realm of "self", we leave our life with God behind because we have taken the wrong fork in the path and are walking the path to self, leading to the life of self. Self-love and self-seeking are the very essence of catering to our flesh man, and lead to a life of pride, lust of the eyes, and lust of the flesh. Therefore, the devil is never absent from them, nor without power in them. However, if we renew our minds with the Word of God, we can be sure-footed in Him as Psalm 119:105 teaches – Your word is a lamp to my feet and a light to my path. And as Romans 2:8 says – but to those who are **self-seeking**, and don't obey the truth, but obey unrighteousness, will be wrath and indignation.

Upon the battlefield of our human mind, two masters are ever battling for the crown of supremacy over our lives, for the kingship and dominion of our heart. They are the master of self, called also the "prince of this world", in other words, the devil, and the "Prince of peace", our Jesus. In every soul the battle is waged, and as a soldier cannot engage in two opposing armies at the same time, so every heart is either enlisted in the ranks of self or in the army of

God with Jesus as the Commander in Chief. There is no half-and-half course. There is self and there is Jesus and where self is, Jesus is not, and where Jesus is, self is not. Jesus declared that "No man can serve two masters; for either he will hate the one and love the other; or else he will hold to the one and despise the other. You cannot serve God and Mammon."

Jesus is Truth and the Truth sets us free. Self is imaginative, crooked, and governed by desire and lust. The deceived worshipers of self vainly imagine that they can gratify every worldly desire, and at the same time, still possess Jesus against worldliness and self-seeking. Jesus declared that he who would be His disciple must "deny himself daily." Are you willing to deny yourself, to give up your lusts, your prejudices, and your opinions? If so, you will find that peace from which the world is shut out. The denying of self is the perfecting path God takes us on so that we strive for perfection in Him. Self is the denial of Jesus and therefore under the influence of the spirit of antichrist, self causes us, by default, to be a child or seed of the devil. Jesus is the denial of self. If you cling to self, Jesus will be hidden from you because the blind and wayward self cannot perceive Him. But if you forsake self, Jesus is the Light and is not hidden. In the earthly realm, the light of day is not hidden to anyone, except to the blind, and in the spiritual realm, the light of Jesus is not hidden except to those who are blinded by self.

We really must beware of our flesh and the deceptions the devil tries to bring us. Remember, the devil only has the authority that we give him. He was stripped of his power over us when Jesus defeated him like Colossians 2:15 says – Having disarmed principalities and powers, He made a public spectacle of them, triumphing over them in it. And in turn, Jesus gave that power and authority to us. The only power the enemy has over us now is in trickery, deceit, and temptation. But he can only do what God allows Him to do. He's a pawn, a tool, a vehicle that God uses in order to reveal a flaw or weakness in us, so that we may realize it, overcome it, and grow stronger in the Lord, becoming a bit more perfected as we press toward the mark.

We need to understand that it's just a training exercise for us when and if we give in to the trickery and temptation of the devil, just like with King David, a man after God's own heart. God's purpose in that is to show us a weakness we need to overcome. In our weakness, He is made strong. God indeed then takes what the enemy meant for evil and turns it around for our own good and for God's own good purposes if we turn and repent. Romans 8:28 says – And we know that **all** things work together for good to those who love God, to those who are the called according to *His* purpose. The only power the enemy has is that which God gives to him to fulfill God's own good purposes toward us and the only way the devil has power over us, is if we give it to him. And now, let's read what Revelation 3:10 says. Here, Jesus is speaking to the faithful church – "Because you have kept my command to persevere, I also will keep you from the hour of trial which shall come upon the whole world, to test those that dwell on the earth." Hallelujah!

We can turn to Jude and see what is happening in our world today. Jude verses 4,7,8, 16-19 – For certain men have crept in unnoticed, who long ago were marked out for this condemnation, ungodly men, who turn the grace of our God into lewdness and deny the only Lord God and our Lord Jesus Christ…as Sodom and Gomorrah, and the cities around them in a similar manner to these, having given themselves over to sexual immorality and gone after strange flesh, are set forth as an example, suffering the vengeance of eternal fire. Likewise also these dreamers defile the flesh, reject authority, and speak evil of dignitaries…These are grumblers, complainers, walking according to their own lusts; and they mouth great swelling words, flattering people to gain advantage. But you, beloved, remember the words which were spoken before by the apostles of our Lord Jesus Christ: how they told you that there would be mockers in the last time who would walk according to their own ungodly lusts. These are sensual persons, who cause divisions, not having the Spirit. And speaking of divisions, I personally know of no "doctrine" within the church that causes more division than that of the tribulation of the Book of Revelation. Think pre, mid, and post arguments.

In this present age, many desire to be leaders for reasons much too similar to those of Nebuchadnezzar back in his day. They desire to rule. They don't want to serve others but to be served. They're not unlike many Christians today who seek to lead, not to serve, but to have status and to be served. Those who are given positions of power and prestige need to beware of pride, being constantly reminded that leadership is both God-given and a manifestation of His greatness—not our own. They need to be mindful of humility. Jesus said in Matthew 23:12 – "And whoever exalts himself will be humbled, and he who humbles himself will be exalted." And Isaiah 14:13-14, speaking of Nebuchadnezzar says – "For you have said in your heart: '**I will** ascend into heaven, **I will** exalt my throne above the stars of God; **I will** also sit on the mount of the congregation on the farthest sides of the North; **I will** ascend above the heights of the clouds, **I will** be like the Most High.'"

Lest we think King Nebuchadnezzar was different from any of us today, we should consider that ours is a day in which individuals seek to be sovereign. They want to be self-directed, self-sufficient, self-gratified, and self-governed. They want to be independent, to be the commander of their own souls, and the masters of their own destiny. Perhaps more than any other age, self-hood is the most prevalent intent of humankind. This is the age of self, as the Scriptures foretold of in 2 Timothy 3:1-2 – But know this, that in the last days perilous times will come: For men will be lovers of themselves.... We, separate from God, and like Nebuchadnezzar, want to be "gods". We wish to dethrone the one true God and to enthrone ourselves. Let Nebuchadnezzar be our example of warning and let us humbly bow our knee to Him from whom, through whom, and to whom, all things are. Amen!

Thank you, Father, for the faith that You have given us and for showing us the way to be overcomers in Jesus. We thank you for having a plan from beginning to end and for making the way for us to be triumphant overcomers within it. Thank you for bringing Your revelation to light that we need not be tossed to and fro with every wind of doctrine and philosophy and be led astray to living our lives for ourselves, according to the traditions of men. Thank you for revealing the deception of 666 and the teaching of how not be deceived by it. Thank you for showing us we need not fear. Thank you for giving us Jesus. Thank you for ordering our steps to be on the right path. We give you all the glory and honor and praise, forever and ever, Amen!

CHAPTER 10

THE BOOKS WERE OPENED

As I was going over and proofreading the chapters of this book, a thing I always do, I came to chapter nine. I thought it was the last chapter, but every time I came to the end of it, I got a check in my spirit. This happened several times as I was proofreading it before I realized, the Lord was telling me I wasn't finished. I then asked Him what I hadn't included. He answered me saying, "The books. I write books too. You can find them throughout the Scriptures."

Of course, this sent me on another journey through His Word. And what became of this journey, the things He opened up and revealed to me, once again, blew my mind. And you just know that I am going to share it with you, thus chapter ten. The first thing I did was to search the Scriptures for the words book and books. There are several that really intrigued me. The first one that really caught my attention is found in Malachi 3:16-18 – Then those who feared the Lord spoke to one another, And the Lord listened and heard *them;* So, a book of remembrance was written before Him for those who fear the Lord and who meditate on His name. "They shall be Mine," says the LORD of hosts, "On the day that I make them My jewels. And I will spare them As a man who spares his own son who serves him. Then you shall again discern Between the righteous and the wicked, Between one who serves God And one who does not serve Him."

While reading this, several things came to mind. The first thing is where people feared the Lord and spoke to one another about Him. After reading that, I was reminded of Matthew 18:20. It reads – "For where two or three are gathered together in My name, I am in the midst of them." This makes sense. Since He's in the midst of us when we gather together in His name, that He would hear what we speak. And then He writes what we say in a book of remembrance of us. I think this is totally cool! The Lord is writing about us in a book! The second thing that came to mind was when I read where He said those that meditate on His name. Meditation is a process of our mind, therefore, when we have the Lord in our minds, it is advertised on our forehead just like we learned in chapter six. The third thing that came to mind was when He said then you will be able to discern who serves God and who doesn't. Or in other words, like when Jesus said in Matthew 7:16 – "You will know them by their fruits…" Thank you, Lord.

In Numbers 21:14, I found there was a book I had never heard of before. – Therefore, it is said in the Book of Wars of the Lord…" Wait! What? There is a book recording all of the battles that the Lord has won? Wow! What an awesome thing to have to give them courage when facing a battle or war. I thought to myself that I'd really like to read it. Then I heard the Lord speak, "You have an even better one! It is before you right now." Yes, it is the Bible, hallelujah! It has even more wars and victories than what was written at that time and is about how our victory is in Jesus, and how we battle our flesh and how we overcome and much more! That's when I was reminded in other places in the Scriptures, that it does indeed declare that the battle is the Lord's. 1 Samuel 17:47 – "Then all the assembly shall know that the LORD does not save with a sword and spear; for the battle is the LORD's, and He will give you into our hands." We also have 2 Chronicles 20:15 – And he said, "Listen, all you of Judah and you inhabitants of Jerusalem, and You, King Jehoshaphat! Thus says the LORD to you: 'Do not be afraid nor dismayed because of this great multitude, for the battle is not yours, but God's'" And even Deuteronomy 1:29-30 says it, just a bit differently. – "Then I said to you, 'Do not be terrified, or afraid of them. The LORD your God who goes before you, He will fight for you, according to all He did for you in Egypt before your eyes.'"

There also are numerous other mentions of and references to books throughout the Scriptures, in both the Old Testament and the New Testament. We have...

Psalm 40:7 – Then I said, "Behold, I come; In the scroll of the book it is written of me.

Psalm 56:8 – You number my wanderings; Put my tears into a bottle; Are they not in Your book?

Psalm 69:28 – Let them be blotted out of the book of the living, and not be written with the righteous.

Psalm 139:16 – Your eyes saw my substance, being yet unformed; and in Your book they were all written, the days fashioned for me, when as yet there were none of them.

Daniel 12:1 – And at that time Michael shall stand up, the great ruler who stands for the sons of your people. And there shall be a time of trouble, such as never was since there was a nation, until that time. And at that time your people shall be delivered, every one that shall be found written in the book.

Luke 10:20 - Yet do not rejoice in this, that the evil spirits are subject to you, rather rejoice because your names are written in Heaven.

Philippians 4:3 - And I urge you also, true companion, help these women who labored with me in the gospel, with Clement also, and the rest of my fellow workers, whose names are in the Book of Life.

Hebrews 12:22-23 - But you have come to Mount Zion and to the city of the living God, the heavenly Jerusalem, to an innumerable company of angels, to the general assembly and church of the firstborn who are "registered" in heaven, to God the Judge of all, and to the spirits of the righteous made perfect.

These are not all the Scriptures pertaining to books but are a scant sampling of them. However, next we're going to take a look at some book references in the Book of the Revelation as they are those where the Lord spoke to me and sent me on an incredible journey of revelation. The first one I read was Revelation 3:5 – "He who overcomes shall be clothed in white garments, and I will not blot out his name from the Book of Life; but I will confess his name before my Father and before His angels." When I read this Scripture, I first noticed that Jesus said, "He who overcomes". I thought to myself that this was awesome because the previous chapter He had given me, chapter nine, was indeed about being overcomers. Then I heard the Holy Spirit speak and ask me to read the rest of the Scripture again. So I read, "…shall be clothed in white garments, and I will not blot out his name from the Book of Life; but I will confess his name before my Father and before His angels." Then He asked me why I thought it was important that the overcomers' names were confessed before angels.

At this point my mind began reeling as I searched my memory regarding angels in the Word. It stopped when I remembered reading angels reaped with a sickle. So, I raced over to that Scripture in Revelation. It's about the reaping of the earth's harvest and the reaping of the clusters of the vine of the earth, also known as the grapes of wrath.

Revelation 14:14-16 – Then I looked, and behold, a white cloud, and on the cloud sat One like the Son of Man, having on His head a golden crown, and in His hand a sharp sickle. And another angel came out of the temple, crying with a loud voice to Him who sat on the cloud, "Thrust in your sickle and reap, for time has come for You to reap, for the harvest of the earth is ripe." So, He who sat on the cloud thrust in His sickle on the earth. And the earth was reaped. The first thing I realized was that it was Jesus who was reaping. Then I remembered back in Revelation 7:3, where an angel commanded the four angels not to harm the earth, the trees, or the sea until they had sealed the servants of God on their foreheads. So I thought this must have taken place already. Then I read on.

Revelation 14:17-20 – Then another angel came out of the temple, which is in heaven, he also having a sharp sickle. And another angel came out from the altar, who had power over fire, and he cried with a loud cry to him who had the sharp sickle, saying, "Thrust in your sharp sickle and gather the clusters of the vine of the earth, for her grapes are fully ripe." So, the angel thrust his sickle into the earth and gathered the vine of the earth, and threw it into the great winepress of the wrath of God. And the winepress was trampled outside the city, and blood came out of the winepress, up to the horses' bridles, for one thousand furlongs. Whoa! It is indeed an angel who gathers up the grapes of wrath from the vine of the earth and tosses them into the winepress of God's wrath! I understood why having Jesus confess our names before angels mattered. The angel would know I was not a grape of wrath, but a branch of the true vine, Jesus, and by the Holy Spirit brought forth good fruits!! Thank you, Father! Thank you, Jesus!

When I had finished those thoughts, I heard the Spirit tell me to turn over to Revelation 19 and begin reading at verse 17. So I did. Verse 17 – Then I saw an angel standing in the sun; and he cried with a loud voice, saying to all the birds that fly in the midst of heaven, "Come and gather together for the supper of the great God, that you may eat the flesh of the kings, the flesh of the captains, the flesh of the mighty men, the flesh of horses and those who sit on them, and the flesh of all people, free and slave, both small and great." And I saw the beast, the kings of the earth, and their armies, gathered together to make war against Him who sat on the horse and against His army. (That would be the overcoming saints, hallelujah!) Then the beast was captured, and with him the false prophet who worked signs in his presence, (those signs we have been warned about) by which he deceived those who received the mark of the beast and those who worshipped his image. These two were cast alive into the lake of fire burning with brimstone. And here I stopped reading because the word "image" jumped up off the page as I read it.

I asked the Lord if that is what He wanted me to see while reading these verses. He replied, yes, look it up. So, I did just that. The word image has several meanings. One of them is a literal inanimate image like graven images, the image of Caesar on the coin Jesus was questioned about, and even the image that Nebuchadnezzar decreed that everyone should worship, the one Shadrach, Meshach, and Abed-Nego refused to bow down to. As a matter of fact, the Greek word charagma is used in Revelation for the word "mark". A charagma was the image of the emperor's head that was put on all Roman coins, and all stamps on official documents. The word image also has a meaning pertaining to a likeness of someone else, not inanimate, but a living being. For instance, the Scriptures teach us that Jesus is the image of God. 2 Corinthians 4:3-4 says – But even if our gospel is veiled, it is veiled to those who are perishing, the glory of Christ, who is the image of God, should shine on them. Also, we have Colossians 1:15 – He (Jesus) is the image of the invisible God, the firstborn over all creation.

The Word also tells us that we were created in His image. Genesis 1:26-27 – Then God said, "Let Us make man in Our image, according to Our likeness; let them have dominion over the fish of the sea, over the birds of the air, and over the cattle, over all the earth and over every creeping thing that creeps on the earth." So God created man in His own image; in the image of God He created him; male and female He created them.

And now let's take a look at another meaning of image, the one that relates to the Book of Revelation. This meaning is a spiritual likeness, pertaining to spiritual things. We have Colossians 3:10 – Do not lie to one another, since you have put off the old man with his deeds, and have put on the new man who is renewed in knowledge according to the image of Him who created Him. We have Romans 8:29 – For whom He foreknew, He also predestined to be conformed to the image of His Son, that He might be the firstborn of many brethren. Now let's take a look Romans 8:9 – But you are not in the flesh but in the Spirit, if indeed the Spirit of God dwells in you. Now if anyone does not have the Spirit of Christ, he is not His. We know that when we are conformed to His image, we bear the good fruit of the Spirit and others recognize that we are like Jesus, or Christ like. It's like what Jesus said, that we would be known by our fruits.

There is a flip side to this as well, and that is what the Lord was showing me. Remember when Jesus told the Pharisees that they were of their father the devil because the desires of their father they wanted to do because the truth was not in them in John 8:44? Remember that we learned if we dethrone Jesus from our minds and put ourselves there, that by default we put the devil there? How living for self was in essence making yourself your god and thereby you were worshipping self? How about when the beast caused all great and small to receive the mark of the beast on the foreheads or hands? Remember how we learned that "causes" in that Scripture verse was used in the bringing forth of fruit? With all of that in mind, let's look at Revelation 19:20 again. – Then the beast was captured, and with him the false prophet who worked signs in his presence, by which he deceived those who received the mark of the beast and those who worshipped his image. These two were cast alive into the lake of burning fire with brimstone.

Okay, we have learned that the mark of the beast is 666, man-self-flesh, man = spirit-soul-body or me-myself-and I, and it is worn or advertised on the foreheads and hands, according to what people who serve self think and what they do, by the fruit or works of the flesh which are adultery, fornication, uncleanness, lewdness, idolatry, sorcery, hatred, contentions, jealousies, outbursts of wrath, selfish ambitions, dissentions, heresies, envy, murders, drunkenness, revelries, and the like. (Galatians 5:19-20) And that the devil wants to trick you into serving yourself and becoming your own god. Jesus taught us we cannot serve both Him and self. Paul tells us in Galatians 5:13, that we have been called to liberty but not to use that liberty as an opportunity of the flesh, but rather through love serve one another. Not to serve self. So, when this verse says "and those who worshipped his image" it is speaking about worshipping their own image, the image opposite of Jesus. This is a spiritual image that is being discussed here. We either reflect the image of Jesus as we become more and more like Him, having the mind of Christ, or we reflect the devil's image from within our own by what we think, say, and by the works we do. We are either a child of God or we are a child or seed of the devil, by default. The first prophecy given in Genesis was regarding that serpent of old, the devil, and what God said to him in Genesis chapter 3. Verse 15 says - And I will put enmity between you and the woman, And between "your seed" and her Seed. So those who worshipped his image were worshipping themselves as they reflected the devil's image. Wow! And there you have it.

Let us thank Father God and His Holy Spirit for revealing to us that the mark of the beast is not some kind of secret, bizarre "literal" thing that only some certain Christians, with unique insight, wisdom, and knowledge get to know about, while others do not. God wants us all to know that the mark of the beast displayed on foreheads is merely referencing those who live according to their flesh-self and according to the ideas and philosophies of this world, thereby denying Jesus. That their lives are simply "marked" by agreement with sin and by default, the father of it, the devil. In other words, the mark of the beast is man serving and worshipping self and reflecting that to the rest of the world.

Lastly, let's take a look at the most important Scripture passage regarding books. Revelation 20:12 - And I saw the dead, small and great, standing before God, and books were opened. And another book was opened, which is the Book of Life. And the dead were judged "according to their works", by the things which were written in the books. The sea gave up its dead who were in it, and

Death and Hades delivered up the dead who were in them. And they were judged, each "according to his works". Then Death and Hades were cast into the lake of fire. This is the second death. And anyone not found written in the Book of Life was cast into the lake of fire. We can see here that along with the Book of Remembrance, there must be books written according to our fruit bearing and the works we displayed, showing whose image we worshipped and reflected.

Let us praise and thank His Holy Name that He creates us, loves us, writes about us in books, calls to us and gives us a way of escape as we yield to Him, and causes us to be overcomers! Hallelujah! May we ever continue to reflect His image to those in the world around us. Thank you, Father for Jesus our Redeemer! May we be used to help others erase the mark of the beast from their foreheads and exchange it for the seal of God as we rise and shine His light into the darkness of the devil's deception and bring people into the great harvest escaping the grapes of wrath! Hallelujah! Thank you, Jesus! Amen!

Other titles from Higher Ground Books & Media:

Raven Transcending Fear by Terri Kozlowski

The Power of Knowing by Jean Walters

Forgiven and Not Forgotten by Terra Kern

Through the Sliver of a Frosted Window by Robin Melet

Breaking the Cycle by Willie Deeanjlo White

Healing in God's Power by Yvonne Green

Chronicles of a Spiritual Journey by Stephen Shepherd

The Real Prison Diaries by Judy Frisby

The Words of My Father by Mark Nemetz

The Bottom of This by Tramaine Hannah

Add these titles to your collection today!

http://www.highergroundbooksandmedia.com

HIGHER GROUND BOOKS & MEDIA IS AN INDEPENDENT PUBLISHER

Do you have a story to tell?

Higher Ground Books & Media is an independent Christian-based publisher specializing in stories of triumph! Our purpose is to empower, inspire, and educate through the sharing of personal experiences. We are always looking for great, new stories to add to our collection. If you're looking for a publisher, get in touch with us today!

Please be sure to visit our website for our submission guidelines.

http://www.highergroundbooksandmedia.com/submission-guidelines

HGBM SERVICES IS OUR CONSULTING FIRM

AUTHOR SERVICES

HGBM Services offers a variety of writing and coaching services for aspiring authors! We can help with editing, manuscript critiques, self-publishing, and much more! Get in touch today to see how we can help you make your dream of becoming an author a reality!

*****

We also offer social media marketing services for authors, small businesses, and non-profit organizations. Let us help you get the word out about your book, your projects, and your mission. We offer great rates, quality promos, consistent communication, and a personal touch!

http://www.highergroundbooksandmedia.com/editing-writing-services

Need Bulk Copies?

If you would like to order bulk copies of this book or any other title at Higher Ground Books & Media, please contact us at highergroundbooksandmedia@gmail.com.

We offer discounts for purchases of 20 or more copies. Excellent for small groups, book clubs, classrooms, etc.

Get in touch today and get a set of great stories for your students or group members.

www.ingramcontent.com/pod-product-compliance
Lightning Source LLC
LaVergne TN
LVHW051644080426
835511LV00016B/2483